Lord save us from YOUR FOLLOWERS

Why is the Gospel of Love Dividing America?

Dan Merchant

Thomas Nelson
Since 1798

NASHVILLE DALLAS MEXICO CITY RIO DE JANEIRO BEIJING

Published in Nashville, Tennessee, by Thomas Nelson. Thomas Nelson is a registered trademark of Thomas Nelson, Inc.

"Lord, Save Us…" movie stills by permission of Zacchaeus Film Group
"Come Home Sweet Child" lyrics © 2006 Sam Martin Music
Quotes from The Pythons © 2003 John Cleese, Terry Gilliam, Michael Palin, Terry Jones, Eric Idle and the Estate of Graham Chapman

"The Gospel For Well Intended Idiots…" comic illustrations by Kyle Holvek
"Roger's Story" illustrations by Joel Mandish
Graphics, interview stills and additional art by James E. Standridge
Interior design and typesetting by Kay Meadows

Thomas Nelson, Inc., titles may be purchased in bulk for educational, business, fund-raising, or sales promotional use. For information, please e-mail SpecialMarkets@ThomasNelson.com.

ISBN: 978-0-8499-2109-4
ISBN: 978-0-8499-2082-0 (IE)

Printed in the United States of America

08 09 10 11 RRD 6 5 4 3 2 1

This book is dedicated to all the people I met
along this journey who were willing to share
a little of themselves with me. Thank you for sharing,
listening, provoking, challenging, forgiving, and loving.

I also dedicate this book to my wife, Kara, and my boys,
Nick and Nate, who have supported, encouraged,
and participated in this journey. I am so grateful
to be on this long road of life with you.

Table of Contents

Chapter One

bumper-sticker
C U L T U R E

I think America has become a bumper-sticker culture—we're way too comfortable with one-way communication. We like to tell people what we think, but we don't like to listen, and I fear we've lost the fine art of conversation—which explains why I was standing in Times Square on a late Tuesday night in December dressed like a human bumper sticker. Call this a creative attempt to resurrect dialogue and understanding—or as my wife affectionately put it, "I can't believe you're going to go out in public in that stupid suit just to have a conversation with a stranger." Yes friends, desperate times demand desperate measures.

I should let you know that I was taping my "adventures in conversation"—if I could actually engage people in genuine conversation, whose beliefs might vary from mine, then I wanted some proof for the skeptics.

Crossing Broadway I strode confidently in my Bumper-Sticker Man Suit toward Jimmy the cinematographer, who kept pulling his headphones off and making that "I can't hear anything" face.

"The wireless won't work with all this interference." He shrugged. I followed his hand as he gestured at the plethora of glowing video screens, neon signs, and electronic billboards that define Times Square. I noticed the ABC television studios across the intersection and the MTV studios above me. I was probably not the only guy on the block with a wireless microphone.

"Could be the radios in the taxi cabs," Jimmy thought aloud.

"The interference could be caused by small bursts of evil emanating from MTV," I said with a straight face.

After twenty years of friendship and labor together, Jimmy merely cracked a smile and kept working, "You'll have to go handheld." He pitched me the stick microphone.

I noticed a couple strolling down the wide New York City sidewalk toward us, "We're on," I whispered. My eyes got wide as I gestured at the pair with my eyebrows. It might have looked like a nervous condition to the untrained eye, but Jimmy understood my subtle signal and in a flash he had the camera on his shoulder. Young Jim Bob from Wichita, Kansas, spun his finger in the air to indicate "we're rolling."

As the couple approached they couldn't help but be drawn in by the mesmerizing power of the bumper-sticker suit. Their momentary bemusement was all the opening I needed.

"Hi, can I ask you five quick questions for a documentary film we're making?" The tall handsome man with gray hair and beard, glasses, and a gray jacket—who reminded me a little of Harrison Ford—exchanged a quick glance with his cute, bespectacled companion. "Okay, sure," he answered and introduced himself as Lou.

DAN: How do you think the universe began?
LOU: With a big bang.

DAN: Where do you think you'll go when you die?

LOU: Nowhere.

DAN: Just in the dirt someplace?

LOU: From whence I came.

DAN: Anytime you can work poetry into an answer you're in good shape. All right, third question: Name something Jesus Christ is known for.

LOU: [thoughtful pause] Raising the dead and caring for the poor.

DAN: Those are two pretty excellent feats. Okay, name something the Christian people are known for.

LOU: Today? Selective hatred and intolerance.

DAN: The ball kinda got dropped somewhere along the way?

LOU: Between Jesus and the Christians I think it was dropped a long time ago.

DAN: Okay, last question: I've heard the phrase "culture wars." Do you know what this phrase means?

LOU: The culture wars? Sure, it's secular culture that's based on reason opposed by religious culture based on superstition.

DAN: So following Jesus is a superstition or are you saying religion, in a broad sense, is superstitious?

LOU: Believing in Jesus . . . [Lou breaks up laughing] I don't believe I'm doing this . . . yes, following Jesus as He is followed today, as a religious icon, is superstition. Following Jesus, the man, who is probably, in some way, a Son of God, is not.

DAN: I appreciate the distinction; I see where you're going with that. In conclusion, I'd appreciate it if you'd take a moment to gaze upon my suit. I am Bumper-Sticker Man. Is there a particular emblem or bumper sticker that speaks to you?

Lou took a moment to study the bumper-sticker suit before selecting a favorite.

LOU: Let's see . . . I like "God Spoke and Bang It Happened." I think that fits nicely with Darwin and the Jesus Fish—not a Jesus Fish but a Fundamentalist Christian Fish.

DAN: [laughs] Thanks. The whole idea with this suit, well, it seems to me like complex ideas are being reduced to simple bumper-sticker slogans and that seems good enough for a lot of people. What are you finding?

LOU: I find that I agree with you. Complex ideas are reduced to bumper-sticker statements and there is no conversation between the two extremes that are represented on your costume. I shouldn't say costume—on your clothing, sorry.

DAN: No, I'm not offended by "costume" because we're having an open dialogue; this is how we do it. We're actually having a conversation.

Lou and I shook hands and shared a final laugh. I have to tell you I was exhilarated by this chat with a smart and interesting person . . . who doesn't believe what I believe. I loved that Lou was open to the idea that he and I could enrich our national conversation together by respecting each other and sharing with each other.

In a way, the Bumper-Sticker Man suit was my twist on the time-honored tradition of the believer on the street corner with the sandwich board. You know the classic "Repent or Burn," "Repent Sinner," "Jesus Loves You," and even the more friendly "John 3:16," but somehow, over the years this one-way, one-sided approach failed to foster engagement and mostly just alienated folks he most wanted to connect with. That approach always seemed like, "I have the answer, and you don't. Come over here and I'll tell you why you're screwed up." Even if we do have the answer, do you think anyone is going to listen to that?

And as a believer, a Christian, a guy who loves Jesus, these street preachers would offend me because they assumed I needed them to lecture me, to save me. They never asked where I was coming from, and it didn't seem as though they cared. Well, I wanted to know why the gospel of love was dividing America, and if I was going to find the answer, I would have to do more listening than talking . . . but first I had to get people to talk.

A group of twentysomethings moved loudly down the sidewalk, laughing and shouting. A mischievous looking guy in jeans and a sweat jacket grinned at me as he and his crew waited at the corner for the traffic light. His name was Jeff.

DAN: Can I ask you five quick questions? They're easy.

JEFF: Throw 'em at me.

DAN: How do you think the universe began?

JEFF: Big bang.

DAN: Number two: Where do you think you'll go when you die?

JEFF: Hopefully heaven.

DAN: Number three: Name something Jesus Christ is known for.

JEFF: Magic tricks . . . I mean miracles. No, I mean magic tricks.

DAN: What is your favorite magic trick? Like card tricks? The disappearing goldfish?

JEFF: I'll go with water into wine, my friend. That ain't a bad little trick.

DAN: Number four: Name something Christians are known for.

JEFF: Fanaticism? Is that a word?

DAN: Sadly, yes. Number five: Have you heard this phrase, the "culture wars"? What's with all this us versus them stuff?

JEFF: I don't know, I guess we all don't fit together.

DAN: Pick a bumper sticker . . .

JEFF: I'm gonna go with "Overturn Roe v. Wade." That's a winner.

The Five-Questions approach served two functions. One, it was a quick and playful way to engage people, and two, it quickly set the parameters. Based on how they answered the five questions, I better understood where my new friends were coming from, which allowed me to have a more interesting and fruitful dialogue with them (and, hopefully, they with me). Of course, sometimes the questions turned out more to be something for them to name than questions. But let's not nitpick.

Despite the late hour, Rosie had a bouncy step, a big smile, and great laugh—but this is the city that never sleeps, isn't it? She was in her thirties, wore a colorful knit cap, and was of Jewish heritage.

DAN: Question number one: How do you think the universe began?
ROSIE: The universe began? Hmmm . . . it developed over time.
DAN: All right, number two: Where do you think you'll go when you die?
ROSIE: I think I will probably go away and . . . I think I will no longer be here when I die. And I'll be, hopefully, a good memory for my family and friends.

DAN: Question number three: Name something Jesus Christ is known for.

ROSIE: I'm thinking of . . . being condemned at the cross or however it is we're supposed to say it. I don't know what it was that He was, but I know He was put up on that cross.

DAN: It wasn't much of a picnic, whatever you want to call it.

ROSIE: That was the image I thought of initially so that's what I went with on your question.

DAN: That's excellent. I want to remind you that there are no wrong answers.

ROSIE: Oh, good.

DAN: Fourth question: Name something the Christian people are known for.

ROSIE: Hmm . . . trying to get other people to be Christian would be one answer I'm thinking of. [laughs]

DAN: That's come up once or twice in your days?

ROSIE: I've heard that, yeah. [laughs]

DAN: Lastly, I've been hearing about this thing called the culture wars. Have you heard this phrase?

ROSIE: To be honest, it's not too familiar, but I'm assuming that it has something to do with different religious groups thinking that their position should be the most powerful.

DAN: You know what? Bottom line, you're probably close. I think they're referring to the hot-button issues like abortion rights, gay marriage, whether or not to teach intelligent design in schools . . . what do you make of these skirmishes?

ROSIE: I think, for the most part, that everyone should mind their own business and let everyone do individually what they want to do—as long as they're not imposing their opinion on others.

DAN: A "live and let live" type deal?

ROSIE: I would say so.

DAN: Great, Rosie, thank you.

ROSIE: You bet. Take care. Peace.

The thing about the bumper-sticker suit that stops people is the dichotomy on parade. Most nut jobs on the street who are wearing a ridiculous getup like this only display their own point of view. It becomes clear to any onlooker: *This guy is just going to shove his idea of the world down my throat, and I don't need it.* That wasn't going to work for me; I wanted the bumper-sticker suit to mirror the debate we're having in our country. The suit is an invitation of sorts to anybody who wants to have a conversation. That's why I went out of my way to represent as many points of view as possible with the bumper stickers and emblems. You can see people trying to reconcile why there is a Jesus Fish positioned next to the Darwin Fish, a "Real Men Pray" sat next to "Free Jesus," "Where's My Church, Dude?" contrasted with "Vote Pro-Life," and so on. All the assumptions go out the window: *Hey, whose side is this guy on anyway?* I hoped this playful complication would signal to people that I was "open," I was willing to listen, and my main priority was to jump-start a dialogue in this country.

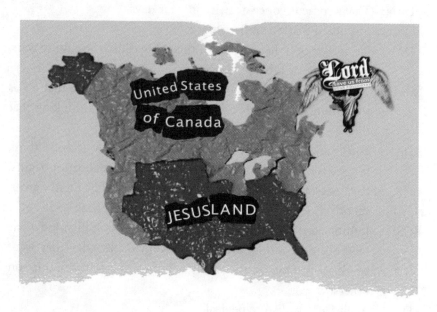

There are some in America who think religious values have gained inappropriate sway in the public square. These folks fear the influence of faith and feel this map defines voting patterns and personal beliefs more accurately than the red-state, blue-state model.

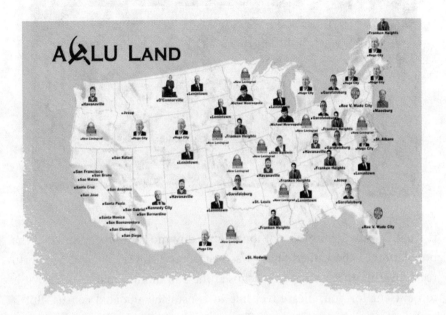

There are others in America who think secular humanism has gained inappropriate sway in the public square. These folks fear that a lack of faith is eroding the values and traditions that have come to define America and in the near future there will be no expressions of faith allowed in the public square. Every city named after a saint will have to change its name! This just in—St. Paul shall now be called New Leningrad.

Nine Out of Ten

Just to prove I did research for this book (and because the numbers are fascinating), I'm sharing with you some basic statistics about our country that I culled from the 2000 U.S. Census Report. By now there may be more current numbers, a 2004 or even a 2008 census of some sort, but the 2000 one

is what I studied, and I'm not looking up any more numbers. In 2000 the population of the United States was pegged at 281,421,906, and I seem to recall hearing that we recently eclipsed the 300 million mark, so if 2000 is too ancient for you, please feel free to consult an updated census. But it really won't make much of a difference and besides they're only numbers and don't reveal the nuances of an individual's belief system. So there! See what happens when I get aggravated? It's not pretty . . . sorry about that.

Okay, so according to the 2000 U.S. Census, 75 percent of the people in the U.S. identified themselves as Christian. The split is about 50 percent Protestant and 25 percent Catholic, and within that number 125 million American citizens identified themselves as born-again or an evangelical—which strikes me as an astounding number! A couple of other sources suggest the total of evangelicals may be closer to 80 million and the National Association of Evangelicals is 30 million members strong, so my conclusion is . . . that's a lot of followers.

Since numbers demand context before any real meaning can be applied, here's a few comparisons for those of you scoring at home: the combined number of atheists and agnostics matches the 2.5 million members of the Missouri Synod of the Lutheran Church, which, coincidentally, is about equal in number to those practicing Native American spiritual traditions.

And while we're playing with numbers, let's add the godless atheists and agnostics together and combine them with the Native Americans and you have roughly five million people, which is about the total number counted in the gay, lesbian, bi-sexual, transgender community. Of course, there is some question as to how accurate the GLBT total in Census 2000 is, since

that specific question wasn't asked, but that's the trouble with a census—the information is limited by whoever is asking the question.

Here is one question that was specifically asked: How often do you attend church? Of the population, about four in ten won't attend church all year and about four in ten will attend more than once this month. So the numbers are tricky: 75 percent checked the Christian box ("Well, honey, I'm obviously not a Hindu, what box do you want me to check?"), but only 40 percent felt strongly enough about their faith to find a church and attend regularly. Of course, I'm not disqualifying your faith if you don't attend church regularly; I'm just saying *numbers lie*.

I hear people on TV ranting about "Nine out of ten people believe in God . . . therefore we should throw Darwin out of school, sing 'Michael, Row Your Boat Ashore' before class, and all vote Republican." The numbers are interesting, don't you think? Nine out of ten Americans believe in the existence of God? And to think we could only get four out of five dentists to come together on that sugarless-gum controversy.

Nine out of ten people, really? (And, hey, I heard this number straight from Diane Sawyer's lips when she was interviewing Mel Gibson on *20/20* when *The Passion of the Christ* had taken the country by storm.) I suspect that of the nine, not all are picturing the God who parted the Red Sea. There's

probably somebody who still believes Clapton is God, though Slowhand has slowed down a bit in recent years (although that Robert Johnson covers album is expertly and lovingly rendered, I have to say).

Maybe this is my own personal issue, but I have a hard time believing a check in the box can tell us anything meaningful. The raw numbers are incomplete, and I needed more detail, hence hitting the streets as Bumper-Sticker Man to ask Americans what they really believe to be true.

DAN: How do think the universe began?

MORGAN: I guess I'm a believer in the Big Bang theory. But, I think if you research it you see how . . . just the idea of that happening there has to be some sort of intelligent force behind it, you know? I do believe in the Big Bang and it taking millions, no billions of years to get here, right?

DAN: I think I have that bumper sticker right here—

MORGAN: "God Spoke and Bang It Happened."

DAN: So maybe? Second question: Where do you think you'll go when you die?

MORGAN: Well, that's the million-dollar question, isn't it? I believe in life after death. What it is I do not know, and I'll probably be wondering that until I find out.

DAN: There's only one way to find it out.

MORGAN: Right? And I hope I don't find it out for a very long time. That will be a question that follows me throughout life.

DAN: Name something Jesus Christ is known for.

MORGAN: Love, right? [laughs] My family is Catholic, but I wasn't raised Catholic. I wasn't raised in the church, but I did have a huge spiritual upbringing. What I was taught, from my mother and my father, was that Jesus Christ and Christianity is based on love. And no one can deny that's a great idea.

DAN: Amen. Number four: Name something that the Christian people are known for.

MORGAN: Politics. I would say, especially in this country, politics.

DAN: Give me an example of some of the things you've seen flying around in the media or in conversations.

MORGAN: Our country is kind of a conundrum because it's built on free-dom of religion, freedom of speech; it's the land of the free—and yet we were founded by a puritan society. But I think the way things are being portrayed today it makes religion feel more political than anything else.

DAN: It feels like, today, complicated issues are being boiled down to their simplest form so it's easier for me to shout what I think at you. It feels like we've lost the ability to have a conversation.

MORGAN: I would agree, I would definitely agree with that and I think it's very sad. I think it's a sick turn this country has taken and, frankly, I'm worried about it. I feel if we don't start getting it together and start listening to each other then I don't like the road we're taking, and I would hate for my children to have to grow up in a country where all we have is walls built up, and rights and wrongs, and no middle ground. You have lots of abortions and Roe versus Wade, which is a big deal right now. You have evolution on your suit and "Inherit the Wind" is going up down the street. . . . We've come so far, but we've taken baby steps to do it and right now we're stagnating. But I think there'll be a push. I have faith in my generation. Yes!

DAN: Is there a bumper sticker that jumps out to you?

MORGAN: Oh, yeah, this one cracked me up, "The Agnostic Dyslexic Insomniac Who Lies Awake at Night Wondering If There Really Is a Dog." That's funny.

To me, the division of America, this separateness, isn't getting any of us anywhere. And both sides are making the same mistake: they think the culture war is a winnable war. Some think, eventually, one side will win out over the other. I don't see it that way. I'm concerned that calling it a culture war presumes a few things, like, if it's a war there is an enemy. This kind of adversarial posture serves to further entrench us in our own posi-tions. The sad fact is, our country is polarized because we like it that way. It is so much simpler to pretend the world is black and white. An "us versus them" attitude is just simpler than critical self-reflection and allows us each to blame the other.

It's funny because I see bumper stickers as a symptom of the disease. A bumper sticker is, quite possibly, the weakest, most strident form of communication possible—because of its one-way nature. In this information age, communication styles are more influential than ever. I've identified four primary ways that have (seemingly) become the accepted ways we communicate our ideas, both through the media and in person.

Myopia—our communication conveys our point of view exclusively. While our facts may be accurate, we lack context and, ultimately, understanding by ignoring any information that doesn't put forward our agenda.

Hyperbole—our communication again conveys our point of view, but we exaggerate the facts and distort the available information to create an intellectually dishonest and, possibly, more persuasive case for our agenda.

Hysteria—our communication conveys our point of view in an emotional and aggressive manner based primarily on our feelings, what we want to be true, and our blind desire to be right and see our agenda come to fruition.

Truth—our communication conveys as balanced a review of the facts as possible, including the weaknesses of our position and the strengths of the other's. The goal of this communication is the illumination of reality and, in this case, our agenda considers the well-being of all people, not just those who agree with us. It's tough to fit this on a bumper sticker.

A balding man in his forties, with a gray trench coat and an attaché bag slung over his shoulder, spent a full five minutes reading the bumper-sticker suit while I talked with a group of twentysomethings from Europe. I noticed him hovering out of the corner of my eye and couldn't decide if he was going to be trouble or not. He had a round, friendly face, bright eyes (which squinted as he pondered various bumper stickers), and a big warm smile. I could tell there was some conflict here, and I hadn't even spoken to him yet. It was already about one in the morning (gotta love NYC), and for a second, I thought about bailing out to avoid this guy (but engagement is what I'm all about, baby!) His name was Jonathan.

JONATHAN: What are you doing?

DAN: A documentary film on the collision of faith and culture, and I have five questions for you.

JONATHAN: Faith and culture . . . but everyone has faith in something, faith in their senses, their intellect—

DAN: I guess I'm referring to faith in God or, specifically, the collision between the Christian faith and a secular culture.

JONATHAN: I know very few Christians who have faith in God. Most of the Christians I've met have faith in the Bible, and most of them have faith in their own mind's interpretation of the Bible.

DAN: So what is true faith then?

JONATHAN: Jesus explained: to love God with all your heart, all your soul, and all your might and like unto that love your neighbor as yourself. That's how He described it. And then in Matthew twenty-five He said, "What you do to the least amongst you, you do unto Me." Now I have yet to see very many people who profess the Christian faith go reach out to the least amongst us. They seem to be aspiring, for the most part, for worldly power.

DAN: Who are you thinking of when you say that?

JONATHAN: I'm thinking of the people who the world calls fundamentalists; I call them exclusivists. The fundamentals of Christianity are really full of love and compassion. And, similarly, the fundamentals of Islam are love and compassion. In this day and age you're even finding exclusivist Buddhists, which is really weird. But this phenomena of using religion to amplify pride rather than humility, to seek power rather than service, and to laud selfish love rather than selfless love . . . people are so preoccupied with their ego-self getting to heaven, I don't know, I read Jesus' doctrine as transcending that self. You see all these ministers, the kind of people our president listens to like Pat Robertson, and their whole preaching is about *you*. You can get saved, and you can be as selfish and self-centered as you want to be. I never saw that in the gospel, or at least not how I read the gospel.

DAN: I think you'd have a hard time finding that in the red letters of the Bible.

JONATHAN: To me, right now, we've got to start defining the values of justice, love, and compassion as universal values and challenge every religion to live up to those values. Because those qualities come from God—they don't come from man, so we have to say to Muslims, "Are you living up to the compassion that Mohammed called you to?" We have to say to Buddhists, "Are you living up to the compassion that Buddha called you to?" And we have to say to Christians, "Are you living up to the compassion that Jesus called you to?" And then we have to say to ourselves, "Are we living up to the compassion God has called us to?" It's time to get beyond the franchises.

Needless to say, I was pleased that I didn't bail out before talking with Jonathan, who, as it turned out, worked for an institute committed to world peace. What a thrill to converse in such an open, dynamic, and positive way. Even after we ran out of videotape, Jimmy and Jonathan and I stood out in Times Square talking about life, God, and America. Every few minutes a person or two would stop on the sidewalk and listen in on our spirited conversation or stop to read the bumper-sticker suit.

Who would've figured that dressing up like a human bumper sticker would've fostered so much good interaction, but, then again, that's what happens if you actually stop and really talk to people.

Chapter Two

There are people who think Jesus is a Republican. My personal feeling is that He probably isn't a Republican, which is not to say I think Jesus is a Democrat. I don't think He is a Democrat either. Perhaps, He is an Independent, but again, that would just be my guess.

When Jesus walked the earth, He lived in an extremely political time; the Romans occupied the land, the local Jewish politicians and religious leaders aggressively jockeyed for position and favor, and Jesus stayed out of it. Many of those sandal-wearing folks who followed Jesus around wondered why He wasn't leading a revolution, as they expected the Messiah to do. The trick was that Jesus did start a revolution, but not in the way many expected. He led a revolution of the heart—a revolution that called for self-sacrifice, kindness, patience, forgiveness, and grace. No wonder they crucified Jesus. Have you tried doing any of those things? It's really hard. Patience and forgiveness? I can totally see how killing a few centurions, burning a palace or two, would be a much more palatable, logical option for them. No wonder those poor, ignorant first-century people didn't get it. What a relief to know how beautifully we've progressed over the ensuing centuries.

There are people who share their views on evolution by plastering their cars with stickers. There are people who picket a gay pride parade rather than spend that same Saturday afternoon volunteering in a soup kitchen. There is a certain practicality to the bumper sticker for it allows the bearer to proclaim his opinion without actually having to listen to anyone else, because, as everyone knows, listening to someone who has a differing opinion is a complete pain in the butt. And I've found it to be quite difficult to share my thoughts with someone when they're talking. With a bumper sticker Driver A can state, "Evolution Is Just a Theory!" and feel quite comfortable that his neighbor has gotten the message. Of course, there is nothing preventing the neighbor, Driver B, from placing a contrary bumper sticker on his car stating, "Evolution Is Just a Theory—Kind of Like Gravity!" I suppose it's possible, eventually, that a conversation might break out between these two car owners; I just hope it doesn't commence while Driver A is prying a Darwin Fish off of the back of Driver B's car. In the interest of full disclosure I should tell you that my wife once placed a Jesus Fish on the back of our Chrysler minivan. But, and this gives you an idea of her wisdom, she also placed a Jesus Fish on the dashboard to remind her of the one on the back of the car.

There are people who go on television to proclaim that the leader of a foreign land suffered a stroke because he made God mad. There are people who blame America's moral decline on activist judges while excusing our selfish, materialistic compulsions. There are people who feel the division in America is justified and inevitable because they are right and the others are wrong. Some of these people write books explaining how uninformed or dishonest the other side is. I wonder sometimes if their books would sell as many if they chose a theme other than "us versus them".

Now, the big problem I have with people such as these is that I share their faith; they're Christians and I'm a Christian. Deep in their being they have a love for the Creator and Savior, just like I do. We worship a god with the same name, we read the same Bible, and so simply to throw them under the bus would be an act of intellectual dishonesty. To be clear, I don't understand why they're saying and acting the way they are, because we share the same faith. That's why I'm confused and a little wound up. I wasn't able to ignore the Reverend Jerry Falwell when he appeared on *The 700 Club* two days after the attacks on the Twin Towers and blamed those attacks on everybody on his political hit list. Among the ones he blamed were the ACLU, secular humanists, and the gays. I didn't see the connection between Islamic extremists who express their faith through terrorism and death and

Falwell's comments—which, while perhaps motivated by grief and impotency, came off as opportunistic. The national news media pounced on him, venting just as he had done. I cringed as that quote flew around the country, and I found myself in any number of uncomfortable conversations: "See, that's why I hate Christians. He's so judgmental and hateful. What do the gays have to do with this?" I had to swallow my tongue. My friends didn't want to hear about the charity work Falwell's organizations do, they didn't want to hear anything about a man they saw as hateful and bigoted. The part that hurt the most was that many take comments like that one and assume Falwell was speaking for all Christians, for Jesus Himself. I don't understand what Falwell was doing that day; I hope he wasn't simply using the tragedy for political traction. And because Falwell loved Jesus as I do, rather than simply dismiss someone I disagree with, I'm willing to dig a little deeper, ask a few more questions.

But sorting through these kinds of comments from fellow believers has become an all-consuming occupation.

I wasn't able to ignore Pat Robertson when he called for U.S. special forces to "take out" Venezuelan President Hugo Chavez. Sure, economically speaking, assassination is cheaper than full-scale invasion, but I'm a little hazy on where Jesus would come down on that question. I'm guessing He'd say, "Assassination or invasion? You're asking the wrong question, son." Wasn't Dr. Robertson aware his sound bite would be on CNN, MSNBC, and Fox News by lunchtime? Those guys have to fill twenty-four hours of airtime each day; they probably have a guy with a tape deck monitoring *The 700 Club* just waiting for something outrageous to be said. In the past few years, Pat has been particularly reliable. Personally, I enjoyed the prediction that a tsunami would hit the Pacific Northwest last year. I live in the Northwest so that resonated with me.

Pat isn't really a fortune-teller in the boardwalk gypsy kind of way, but he does an annual retreat where he meditates and prays and God gives him the straight stuff. I believe God talks to us. I believe that God puts things on our heart, and we do our best to translate the message or comprehend it properly. Personally, on the few occasions when I've felt God has spoken to me, the message has been so vague or simple that only later did I fully grasp the profundity of the encounter. So when Dr. Pat is told by God a big wave

This Week	Last Week	Sin Name	Peak Position	Weeks On Chart
2	3	Abortion	1	28,987
3	2	Murder	1	12,009
4	1	Assisted Suicide	1	520
5	6	Lying	1	166,280
6	4	Blasphemy	4	56,480
7	-	Sloth	7	32,110
8	5	Stealing	3	275,800
9	8	Don't Covet Your Neighbor's Wife	8	66,690
10	16	Greed	10	19,220

is going to whack my home state, I'm skeptical about the level of detail in such a message—but that's only based on my personal experience. The biblical word for this kind of give-and-take with God is *prophecy*. Interestingly, when an Old Testament prophet foretold a prophecy and was wrong, he was stoned to death. Should be easy for me to throw Pat under the bus, right? Wrong. Pat is also the guy who has used television to deliver the Word, not all of it whacked, to millions who may not otherwise have heard it. His affiliated nonprofits (there's a pun in there somewhere, but I'll let you do the math), including Operation Blessing, did enormously important relief work in the aftermath of Hurricane Katrina. Again, I'm conflicted, especially when I consider all the stupid, opinionated things I've spouted through the years. The difference, I suppose, is that my stupid comments have offended and alienated friends and family, who eventually will forgive and forget. Pat manages to say plenty of silly things live on national television and, besides,

I'm supposed to love Pat—even if I don't agree with him. Can you love someone and still throw him under the bus? There must be a scripture verse somewhere that covers this.

I wasn't able to ignore Dr. James Dobson when he claimed that gay marriage could mark the end of Western civilization, that polygamy and men marrying dogs would come next. I wondered if the "slippery slope" analogy is where Jesus would go with that complicated legal issue. I also wondered if Jesus would care about the end of Western civilization. And by Western civilization, I mean our American privilege, our comfort, my cozy do-whatever-I-want-buy-whatever-I-want way of life. I know Jesus cares about each and every heart, but many empires have risen and fallen since Jesus walked the earth. I can't imagine protecting our castle is what Christ had in mind. But Dr. Dobson has written a couple of excellent books on raising children that were helpful to my wife and me in raising our boys. Through the years, I've spent many hours listening to his radio program on topics like family dynamics and have been truly blessed by those shows. Again, there's the rub. I'm not going to sign on with Dobson on his Culture Wars Cruise through America, and I'm concerned that too much preaching to the choir will alienate those we're called to love and share. I don't know what to do with this dichotomy, but the queasy feeling in my stomach isn't going away.

Over the past couple of election cycles, I've watched the division grow sharply between Christian and non-Christian, conservative and liberal, blue-stater and red-stater. And, hey, I'm fine with good old-fashioned politics. But I have to say I was not sold when religious leaders told me how to vote. None of them *know* how Jesus would vote, if He would vote. Oh sure, they'll tell you why they *think* Jesus would vote with them, but nobody knows. I could tell you Jesus would like the Beatles more than the Rolling Stones because the Fab Four wrote so many songs about love, but I don't *know*. Perhaps Jesus would be a big fan of the blues-based Stones because the music expresses the sadness, pain, and emptiness that only Jesus can fill. Maybe Jesus loves the blues because it's honest and the desperation is a call for help; it's the musical equivalent of the dirty, sick, undesirable loners Jesus came to love. Check one for the Stones? We can't really *know*, can we?

The sweeping "values voters" win in 2004 brought a round of gloating and heavy-handed, myopic policy demands and a lot of talk about how

God had decided this election. Now, while some of the candidates I supported won, some didn't. Some of the ballot measures I supported won, some didn't. I was watching our democratic election process through a different filter than some of my outspoken brothers. I found myself getting irritated that they were so sure God had delivered these election results. *Well,* I thought, *He didn't deliver all of my desired outcomes. Does that mean I'm less holy than you? Does that mean I'm wrong and you're right? Does that mean you have God on your side and I'm out in the cold?* I could only imagine how someone outside the faith must feel when he hears this kind of rhetoric.

Then something hit me, *These guys don't have any idea how they sound.* The negative association with Christianity is being helped along because we don't know how we sound. Christianity is turning into a bad word with dubious meaning in American society because we don't care how we sound to those who don't agree with us. There are many believers who, and they have their reasons, feel like we must "Take Back America from the Godless Secularists." There is pent-up aggression that has exploded in this country and is manifest in an ongoing collision of faith and culture. Some have joined the fray out of deep-seated religious beliefs, some out of political convictions; for some it's good business, and some—as we've seen—have good old-fashioned agendas such as the quest for power and money. All of that is as American as a McDonald's hot apple pie and baseball's free agency, but there is some question in my mind where Jesus fits into this whole thing. That seems like a good place to start: Are we trying to fit Jesus into what we're doing as people, as a country? Or are we trying to fit into what Jesus is doing?

As believers, I think we simply don't know how we sound to others; what's worse, we don't care 'cause we're right anyway—and to add insult to injury, we won't listen. What if, with all our talking, people aren't actually hearing what we intend? If we listened for a minute, we might understand how "I want to preserve the traditional institution of marriage" comes across as "I hate gay people." So what if we don't think that's what we're saying. If that's what others are hearing, what's the difference? I can't be concerned with whose fault it is—I can't accept this communication breakdown. Should the burden be on my lips or their ears? I guess it depends on whether I really want to have a conversation or I simply want to be right.

On a wet fall Sunday a few weeks after the 2004 elections, I was walking through my church parking lot, running late to the eleven o'clock service. I know it's lame to be *late* to the late service, but I was. As I approached the church, I noticed a slightly beat-up, '70s era Chevy Impala, which in the used-car selling game would be politely marked "high miles." There were several bumper stickers plastered over the back half of the car, but my eyes locked on to one in particular: "Lord, Save Us From Your Followers." I stopped walking and laughed. It was so refreshing to see this bumper sticker on a car in a church parking lot. Had I seen this car in a parking lot at a ball game or a rock concert it wouldn't have carried the same impact. I loved it that a churchgoer wasn't afraid to tweak a nose or two by slapping that doozy on his car bumper.

Amen, I thought. *Those Followers are killing me.* My mind raced over all the outspoken, angry, strident believers that I'd been hearing and reading about. They had won their election, but I could feel the frustration and resentment of others building up. Heck, I had frustration and resentment and was having a hard time reconciling this prevailing attitude with Jesus' call to "love one another" and "to forgive seventy times seven" and to "love our enemies" and to "turn the other cheek." There were a lot of folks claiming Jesus was on their side who didn't remind me of Jesus at all. I realized the "love one another" thing can be pretty annoying. My version of that axiom is much simpler to follow: "Love one another . . . unless they irritate you." Now, maybe I'm wrong. Maybe I'm missing something and so instead of just dismissing these Followers, I wanted to learn more, dig deeper. It's too easy to sit back and criticize things you don't know about and much more difficult to search for truth—and, yes, I'm applying that to myself first.

As I walked away from that bumper sticker, something else stirred in me—I imagine it was God tapping me on the shoulder—a realization that far too many people have been one of those Followers and I have been one of *them* too. My heart sank. I had to admit there have been far too many instances where my selfishness, impatience, ignorance, arrogance—you name it—has pushed people further away from God rather than closer to Him. It's a bummer to realize I am one of *them*. It's kind of a drag to realize I am part of the problem—it's much easier simply to blame those I don't like. Do you recognize yourself as one of *them* too?

So, yeah, I guess maybe God spoke to me through a bumper sticker. A few ideas began to articulate from raw feelings I'd been wrestling with for some time. For one, I became acutely aware of just how exhausted I was by the division in our country. I guess this had been wearing on me and explained why I was so irritated by the evening news and cable news channels and *Time* and *Newsweek* and the morning newspaper. I knew something was wrong and found myself impatient, hypercritical, and mostly disgusted when I saw believers talking loud and proud about how God was on their side of the argument. Maybe I was exhausted by the idea that this division is acceptable or inevitable. I can't believe what I believe and accept that. I've heard people mockingly quote Rodney King's "Why can't we just get along?" as if it's something totally unattainable. Maybe it is "unattainable" (we're humans, we're fallen, I get it), but the alternative of not trying or just adopting a selfish agenda strikes me as downright ghoulish. Is this defeatist attitude all right with Jesus?

If I were to sit down for tea with Jesus, I would not feel comfortable saying, "Hey, Lord, listen, this whole 'love one another' thing isn't working for me."

"You mean my new commandment?" Jesus smiled.

"Yeah, dude. That one is super hard. Besides, there were already the Ten Commandments; did we really need a new one?" I'd protest.

"I was thinking this one wrapped them all together," the Savior would reply between sips of tea.

"Yeah, I don't know, with the ten I can sort of pick and choose and feel good that I obeyed like, seven or eight, which out of ten is pretty good." I wasn't going down easy.

"I am afraid you may be missing the point," He reached across the table and put a gentle hand on my shoulder. "The ten are for you, gifts to remove the burden from your journey; the new commandment is the journey. If you want to show Me you love Me and you love your heavenly Father, show Me by loving My people."

I'd nod and smile, trying to comprehend what He was saying. Then I'd "accidentally" spill my tea all over my lap in order to change the subject.

Tolerance is a word that gets bandied about by everyone in the culture wars these days. I'd like to propose we should be intolerant to separation and division from others. Now, I'm not talking about making friends with Iran. They're clearly evil, a threat to stabilization in the Middle East, a danger to the West, and I've heard they want to drink the blood of the "infidels" (which is us). So they're off the list, but everyone else we should love. *Kidding.* Did I get you for a second? See? Clearly, the Iranians are too far away to be a real threat.

I should've said it's the gay Darwinist sex-ed teachers in our schools; those are the ones it's okay to hate. Their subtle infiltration into our way of life can only mean destruction. *Kidding.* People, please, stay with me here. Jesus' call is painfully simple and majestically difficult: "Love one another." Realistically, I think the parenthetical should read, "Love one another." (Yes, I mean *them,* did you think this was going to be a cakewalk?) It's possible there is a new, hip translation that properly updates the original Greek. (Or was it Aramaic? Hey, I'm an observer of and participant in the culture wars, not some kind of first-century rocket scientist.)

The point is, it's easy to make exceptions to Jesus' call. Now I'm not trying to be a jerk here; I'm merely illustrating how flipping easy it is for *us Christians* to disqualify someone or some group. We declare them unworthy . . . unworthy of our best . . . unworthy of the love we're called to share. That is simply unacceptable. I don't think it's right to partake of this faith *and* blame others for this tumult. You know, that whole "He who is without sin . . ." thing weighs on me. And since none of us are in the "No Sin Zone," aren't we all in the same predicament?

I tend to get confused, so I want to be sure I'm articulating my thoughts as clearly as intended. Let me see if we're tracking together, okay?

Christians are the ones who believe in the God of love, right? We're the ones who love and worship the Prince of Peace, right? Isn't that us? Aren't we the ones who are to hold patience, kindness, and forgiveness up as ideal standards? We're the truth and grace people, correct? Then why are we hammering others with the truth (our take on it, anyway), and then neglecting to share the grace? Those two things go together; one doesn't mean as much without the other.

Why are we so comfortable blaming those who disagree with us for the conflicts in our country? Why are we allowing the gospel of love to divide America? I'm comfortable with the bar being higher for us. If not us, then who? We're saved, right? Isn't that worth something now? Jesus is the one who accepts everybody, who includes the weakest in His embrace, restores the broken, desperate, and unworthy (there I go again, trying to sneak one by you . . . yes, you're right, we're all unworthy, that's why I'm so grateful for grace). If we are truly to represent Him, we better come up with a better plan than dividing the country over temporal, political issues.

I saw a news magazine interview with Billy Graham, who back in the day was quite politically active. He counseled and prayed with presidents, took major stands on current political issues, and now near the end he looks back with regret on pouring so much energy into politics. I found it fascinating that Graham felt that he should have always kept the emphasis on Christ's love, because everything else fades. They say "hindsight is twenty-twenty"; they also say "history repeats itself"—there must be a way to combine those two axioms into something relevant to the so-called culture wars.

I thought about the bumper sticker, "Lord, Save Us From Your Followers," which started to sound like a prayer to me—not a cheap joke. "Lord . . ."—the writer calls out reverentially to the Almighty, "Save Us . . ."—a call for protection that is not selfish or exclusive, "From Your Followers . . ."—the author expresses an inability to communicate or connect with the Followers, apparently something only the Master of all time, space, and dimension is capable of doing. (You weren't expecting this level of scholarship in a book named after a bumper sticker were you? Well, friends, prepare to be repeatedly shocked and amazed.)

But there was another message embodied in this bumper sticker: beware of oversimplification. I spent much time analyzing that silly bumper sticker and gleaned profound meaning from it (sounds crazy, but stay with me here). It serves as a symbol of how our culture oversimplifies the complex issues at the heart of the conflict. We are so comfortable with slogans and catchphrases we've forgotten they're only symbols to quickly and simply communicate a larger issue or position. We've been so used to talking in this consumer-culture shorthand that the actual meaning behind the slogans has slipped away. "Evolution Is Just a Theory," a common bumper sticker, can't be your *entire* position on this subject; we can't accept such radical over-simplification and do justice to the conversation. "God Said It and That's It" is going to fall a tad short of conveying the expansive totality of the Creator to someone who is skeptical. And for us to be okay with offering so little to others is just not going to cut it. I'm sorry, but we've done a crummy job of communicating to those who don't understand where we're coming from. Our tendency to reduce the gospel of Jesus to a couple of isolated issues, our willingness to oversimplify this complex life just so we can be right and win an argument is, as a smart person would say, antithetical to Jesus' teachings.

This is my theory anyway, my working assumption, let's call it a place to begin. I'm open to the fact I may have read too much into that "Lord, Save Us From Your Followers" bumper sticker, but I did have this tangible reaction to that experience. The tug in my gut felt real: *this isn't how it's supposed to be and you are not supposed to sit here idly waiting for things to change.*

Why Is the Gospel of Love Dividing America?

If I had to boil it down to one question that would be it. This is where the contradiction lives. If I could figure out what part of the gospel (or perhaps, how we represent it) is doing the dividing—if it even is—then I'd find my answer.

Maybe there's a good reason why things are how they are. Maybe I'm missing something. I also have a longing to connect with people who think I hate them. I have a longing to meet people where they are, the way Jesus did. I have a longing to share Jesus' love with others so they can know Him and He can see that I'm trying to love Him as best I can . . . even if I do name my book and movie *Lord, Save Us From Your Followers*.

Chapter Three

red-letter

C H R I S T I A N

Why is the gospel of love dividing America?

I figured the best way to get to the bottom of this cultural divide was to ask the people who were already in the midst of this cultural divide, the Followers who are out in front of the constituencies standing up for what they believe. Well, I put out interview requests to about everybody you could imagine and to my delight the first "yes" was from Dr. Tony Campolo. You may know him by name, maybe you don't, but he's been around the issues of social justice for as long as I've been alive, maybe longer. As a college professor, Campolo has been a diligent educator for decades; as an author, he's told us stories that help us reconcile our faith with this culture; as a speaker, he challenges believers to live up to our beliefs. His book *Let Me Tell You a Story* is full of brilliant, faith-affirming anecdotes and is frequently quoted by American pastors. (I guarantee someone you know has retold one of his anecdotes.) And Campolo's book *Letters to a Young*

Evangelical takes a passionate, thoughtful approach to the culture wars. On a recent television appearance, Campolo was introduced by Comedy Central's Stephen Colbert as a "liberal evangelical," which Colbert noted was an oxymoron.

DAN: We're doing a piece called "Lord, Save Us From Your Followers" that we hope is equal parts outreach to people who are outside the faith who have kinda gotten the wrong idea, because we gave 'em the wrong idea—

TONY: That's right.

DAN: and equal part admonition to us as believers. So let's talk about politics a little bit. I'm hearing a lot of "Let's take back America" business, and the guys who are shouting the loudest are people who seemingly believe the same stuff I believe. Yet I can't seem to get past this angry posture. There is something that feels weird to me about it. What do you see going on?

TONY: That this country was founded on certain biblical principles of human dignity is without question; secularists will say that as well as religionists. There's a fear in this country, and I think it's a legitimate fear, that a group of people believe that they have a right to take over America and control it in accord with their values and in accord with their lifestyles. And there are people saying, "But their values aren't our values and their lifestyles aren't our lifestyles. If they take over are they going to impose their ways on us?"

We have to consider how we sound to others. Look back at Tony's last response. He was talking about how other people are in fear of Christians. Seems odd doesn't it? Aren't *they* the ones messing up *our* country? I can come up with a bunch of justifications why I'm right and these scaredy-cats need to cowboy up and get out of my way. But this does nothing to bring us closer together and the impasse remains. Let us consider the other side for a moment. When Tony talks about a group being scared of values and lifestyles being imposed, imagine for a moment he's talking about conservative Christians being afraid of a homosexual agenda coming to power where certain lifestyle choices would be imposed on us. How would you feel about that? Not great, right? We might become a little agitated and hostile. If we can understand how the other side feels, perhaps we'll choose our words more carefully. If we want to communicate our point of view, engage in a dialogue, we'll do more than simply shout our point of view.

TONY: There's a triumphalism in certain segments of the religious community, particularly the Religious Right, that says, "We're going to conquer America and we're going to impose our will on the masses." It's almost as though there's a fear that what happened in Iran—with the Ayatollah coming into a hitherto secular society with a religious lifestyle forcing people who weren't ready for this to accept it—will happen here. Of course, it's not going to be anything like that because Islam is very different from Christianity. But having said that, there is that fear and people legitimately raise the question, How is this going to affect the rest of us?

DAN: But the Religious Right, or evangelicals, or however you want to put it, feel that they're right about this, that they have God and the Constitution on their side. You were right, Tony, history says, about the stance on equality and civil rights in the 1960's, but intellectually that was still one side pushing their views—unpopular views in some parts of the country—on the rest of us. How is this different?

TONY: All during the sixties there was an attempt by certain people, who had liberal social ideas about race and women, who said, "We feel we can use the instrument of government to impose our values on the general population." The difference (between then and now) would be this: Those of us in the sixties who were championing for civil rights, the rights of women, etc., were saying, "This is in harmony with the Constitution. This is in harmony with the values that are inherent in law." Martin Luther King Jr. stood up and said, "All I am asking is for America to be faithful to the things that it says in the Constitution." There is a sense right now that the line between the separation of church and state is getting blurred. People are trying to use the state to impose religious values that are beyond the realm of the Constitution, not to impose the justice principles of the Constitution. That's the difference between the two.

DAN: People outside the faith, people outside of Christianity, seem to be getting a distorted view of what this faith is. If you were to hear certain comments from Jerry Falwell or Pat Robertson or James Dobson on certain occasions and compare that to the Gospels . . . do you see why people might get confused?

TONY: Yes, I do see why people get confused. It seems to me when the Christian community, when the evangelical community, takes a strong pro-life stand, the rest of the world says, "Okay, we understand where you're coming from. We understand why your religious values and beliefs motivate you to take such positions." They understand that. What they don't understand is how people who call themselves evangelical Christians can support capital punishment in face of a Jesus who says, "Blessed are the merciful for they shall obtain mercy." Who calls upon us to return good for evil. Who presents a philosophy of restitution and reconciliation rather than retribution. They don't understand that. They also don't understand the very pro-war mind-set of the evangelical community. They're stunned when they see the evangelical church drape the American flag over the cross, as I have seen on the front of three churches lately. They're saying, "It seems strange to us that people who follow the greatest peacemaker of all time should be so pro-war, so militaristic." This leads to labeling people who have questions about the war as not only "unpatriotic," which would be bad enough, but "unchristian."

DAN: If we are called to love the lost, do we get to decide who is in and who is out? That's how it looks to people.

TONY: They have a hard time understanding the position that the evangelical community takes on an issue like, say, homosexuality. Now, they understand perfectly well that given certain biblical requirements, evangelicals have to be opposed to gay marriage. What they can't understand is why they think gay marriage would be bad for people who aren't Christians. The gay people want to know, "How are we hurting you? We're living together, devoted to each other. We have a white picket fence. We want to adopt children. We pay our taxes. How are we hurting you? Now, you have a right to say we're living out of the will of God, and that our behavior is sexually unacceptable given biblical principles, but this is a free country. Why do you want to take rights away from us?" These are the sorts of things that are concerns for many who are outside the church.

DAN: I can see how people are confused when conservative Christians are pro-life and pro-capital punishment.

TONY: If you were to take a poll on capital punishment, where do you think you'd find more support: among the secular humanists at Harvard or the evangelicals at Bob Jones University? The answer is obvious. You'd have more support in the Christian circles, and the secular world is saying, "We're having a hard time understanding that, given the New Testament." And of course the most important thing is, they can't understand how the Christian community can support political administrations that are committed to giving tax breaks to rich people while poor people are getting the ground cut from under them. Seems to us that the Jesus of Scripture was very committed to the poor. I can see the point of view of those who say, "This is the responsibility of the church; it's not the responsibility of the state." I would differ with that. We have the right to call upon the nations. It's interesting to note that the twenty-fifth chapter of Matthew, which everybody likes to cite when dealing with the poor, "I was hungry, did you feed me? I was naked did you clothe me? I was sick, did you care for me?" ends with these words: "And on that day I judge the nations." The nations! He doesn't say, "On that day I shall judge the church." Jesus says, "I'm gonna judge the nations." Check it out in Scripture.

DAN: There are many who agree the poor need to be tended to, but who should do it?

TONY: Yes, now my moderate friends would say, "We don't question that the Bible talks a great deal about the poor. We just don't think it's the task of the government to take care of the poor. They shouldn't be taking tax dollars and taking care of the poor. The care of the poor is something Christ called His people to do, therefore it's the responsibility of the church to care for the poor." And there's a lot to be said for that particular point of view; I think it's a very viable point of view. The question is, what do we do about things like health care? Can churches handle that, considering the cost of health care in America? What are we going to do about universal education for the poor? Can the church do that? Can the church come up with the assets to respond to the AIDS crisis in Africa, which will cost billions and billions of dollars? Can the church do that and still maintain its mission? So you can see how the argument goes.

In our culture, perception seems to equal reality. The word *Christian* now comes with some rather dubious baggage. Add the word *born-again* or *evangelical* in front of the word *Christian* and many Americans will assume you are a Republican who hates gays, abortionists, and the ACLU. The perception of our faith is not particularly flattering and seems to be based on what we're against rather than what we stand for. And in this bumper-sticker culture, sometimes what the label communicates is our only opportunity to enter the conversation. I have a friend with dual Canadian/American citizenship. When he travels overseas, which passport do you think he uses? Yep, Canadian . . . less baggage to carry, right? And I get it. When I identify myself to people as a Christian, I have to be ready to answer for the outlandish comments made by fellow believers. No doubt you've found the same things. This dynamic is no different for Tony Campolo, but and he and some friends came up with an interesting solution.

TONY: A group of us who are Christian communicators, who are all evangelicals, got together in Washington and we said, "What do we call ourselves? We don't want to call ourselves Religious Right, 'cause that's not where we are. We don't want to call ourselves Religious Left because that's not where we are." We finally went with a name that was given to us by a secular, Jewish, country and western disc jockey in Nashville, Tennessee, who referred to us as people he liked because we were "red-letter Christians." Red-letter? What does that mean?"

He answered, "Well if you get that Bible, in the New Testament there are certain verses in red. Of course, they're the words of Jesus. You guys are really into the words of Jesus. That's what I like."

So there's the issue. Are we going to stick with Jesus? Or are we going to go with the agenda of those who raise questions about helping the poor? Because Jesus speaks a great deal about helping the poor.

DAN: Doesn't America contribute the most money of all the industrialized nations? I mean as a gross number, maybe not as a percentage.

TONY: Well to put it in perspective, for every dollar America gives, the people of Norway give seventy out of their national budget. Now there are other ways in which we give; we give through missionaries, private donations, a tsunami comes along and we give emergency relief, but in terms of the federal budget we should do more.

DAN: With the work Bono is doing with the ONE Campaign and Rick Warren's efforts in Africa, it would seem that we're doing some things right.

TONY: There is no doubt that there is an awakening in the evangelical community, particularly that caring for the poor is a biblical obligation. You mentioned Rick Warren, and he would be a good example. He says now, "I went through seminary. I have doctorate degrees. I've been a Bible student for years. How could I have missed all of these passages of Scripture that talk about caring for the poor?" And, of course, he's getting his church people directly involved in meeting the needs of poor communities all over Africa and doing it brilliantly. But, once again, there are those who say, "We approve of that, that's a church living out Christ's commands for the poor. What we object to is taking tax dollars and doing it." I contend for both. I contend the needs of the world are such that the nations have an obligation as well as the church.

DAN: There are issues like the Christmas tree versus holiday tree, intelligent design versus evolution, and gay marriage. These issues have Christians running around with their hair on fire.

TONY: [laughs] If they have hair.

DAN: [laughs] Yeah, sorry. Are we focusing on the wrong things?

TONY: The Christmas situation was a good example. The evangelical community, from one end to the other, as far as religious radio and religious TV were concerned, were screaming and yelling over the fact that the president's greeting card coming out of the White House said "Happy Holidays" and not "Merry Christmas." They thought Christ was being taken out of Christmas. I really feel there was a lot made out of nothing. Please don't get me wrong; I think they did have a point. Almost the same thing happened in Lambeth, a city that sits across the Thames from London. They decided to call the Christmas lights "holiday" lights. But it wasn't the Christians who raised the dickens over it—it was the Muslims and the Jews. They said, "If you start taking religious holidays away from Christians, how long will it be before it's Ramadan and Yom Kippur? We're concerned about the trend here." So I think there is a point, but the point was overmade, and may I point out that while we were focusing on those things we missed larger issues. I think the issue of the morality of the war in Iraq is a much more important issue than whether "Merry Christmas" is on the president's holiday card. I mean if you're talking about Christmas, you're talking about peace on earth, goodwill to men and women . . . Jesus came to bring peace. We should be working for peace. It can be argued that we are, but I don't think so. [laughs]

DAN: Well, where does this thing come from then? Is this just a way to generate fear and hold power?

TONY: Here's a great statement—I wish it were mine. It comes from Eric Hoffer who wrote the book *The True Believer.* "A movement can exist without a God but never without a devil. There has to be an enemy to be destroyed." Now, I'm an old guy; my idea of a happy hour is a nap. But I remember when the devil was the Communists. Christian preachers on radio and television would say, "We need your financial support because the Communists in this country are everywhere. They're in Hollywood, they're in our schools, they're in our media, they're in our government, they're in the United Nations . . . they're taking over and we've got to fight them."

All of a sudden one day the Communists were gone. Thanks to Ronald Reagan, say what you will about him, he has to be credited as the primary force to bring down communism. I can still hear him saying, "Mr. Gorbachev, tear down that wall." All of sudden the Communists were gone. To accuse someone of being a Communist meant nothing, and we needed a new devil and we found one, he's called the secular humanist. "They're taking over the whole country. Look what they're doing in the public schools." The National Education Association points out, from a survey, that 72 percent of all teachers inAmerica attend church at least once a month. If I were a secular humanist, I would be scared to death to send my kid to a public school because the influence is so strong there. Even if they don't sing Christmas carols at Christmastime, the general tenor there, the values of most teachers (granted, I can point out the exceptions) are overwhelmingly positive. Instead of attacking the public school teachers and calling them secular humanists, as I hear them doing on Christian radio all the time, we ought to be saying to the public school teachers, "We're going to have a Recognition Night at the church for you. You are the heroes of our society; you work in a difficult environment and, in the words of Saint Francis, 'You preach the gospel all day long, even if you don't say a word.'" We ought to be praising the teachers instead of condemning them, saying, "They're agents of the evil one."

DAN: So is this just a bill of goods to fund ministries?

TONY: Of course it is. I hate to say it, but you have ministries out there that cost hundreds of millions of dollars to maintain. You gotta raise money. Nothing raises money like having a devil that has to be destroyed. "Send us your money, get behind us, support us, and we will lead the fight against the devil out there." You know the interesting thing is the Old Testament prophets were different. They believed there was a devil, but they didn't say, "The devil's out there and must be destroyed." They said, "Let's look within ourselves. The devil is within us." As 2 Chronicles seven says, "If we will confess our sins, if we will get purged of our sins, if we will get rid of the devils in our own lives then all will be well for us." That's what Jesus taught: before you look at the evil out there, in the secular humanist, you'd better take a good look at the evil that is within your own lives.

    And I think it's time for the evangelical community to begin to say, "What's wrong with us?" Let's take a look at our own morality. Let's read through the Sermon on the Mount, let's look at the red letters of Jesus and ask, "Are our values in harmony with the red letters of the Scripture? Are we the meek? Are we the poor?" Let's read in Luke six and ask ourselves, "Are we the people who are merciful? Are we the peacemakers? Are we the ones who are willing to stand up for depressed people even when they say all manner of evil against us? Are we living in accord with the teachings of Jesus?" The enemy is within us, and we need to deal with that enemy before we start looking for the enemy out there in the larger world.

DAN: Why is it so hard for the church to be self-aware and self-critical?

TONY: We're poor at it, but I gotta say this, we're better than any other religion on the face of the earth [laughs]. If you want self-correction, you are more likely to find it in the Christian community than you are in the Islamic community. The fortunate thing about evangelical Christianity is, though they may scream and yell at people like me, they are still willing to keep us within the community. They are still willing to say, "There are some evangelicals who hold views we have to seriously question." I like that because they still acknowledge that I'm an evangelical.

We have to remember that while the church is the instrument to buttress the status quo and resist change, it has also been behind about every positive change you can think of. Would there have been a civil rights movement without the church? Without Martin Luther King Jr.? Would there have been an end to apartheid in South Africa without a Bishop Tutu and the church there? Who is it that championed women's rights? It wasn't a bunch of secular feminists. The first meetings of the Niagara Council were held in churches. The great revivals of the eighteen hundreds were what gave birth to the feminist movement. You know, everybody criticizes us for being people who retard progress, and I argue just the opposite. There wouldn't be much progress in our society, if it wasn't for the church taking the lead. Yes, we have people in the church who are reactionaries, but also we have people in the church who speak the gospel in the fullest sense of liberating the oppressed.

DAN: I can imagine the Religious Right or Dr. James Dobson using those same arguments to defend a stance against same-sex marriage.

TONY: Is the Left willing to sit down with Jim Dobson and have a conversation rather than just condemn him? Both parties have to be open; both parties have to be willing to have a dialogue—or we just end up shouting at each other.

DAN: Yes, being right has become the most important thing.

TONY: We really have to recognize that we're really never as right as we think we are. I can look back on my own life—on positions that I took. I was sure there was no way I could possibly be wrong and later found out I was wrong. There were times too I was convinced I was wrong and I now see that I was right.

DAN: Do we have an arrogance of being right that clouds our priorities?

TONY: I think there is an arrogance to the way we interpret Scripture, that we think our way of reading it, whatever group we're in, is the only way of reading it. Whenever you carry on discussion you always have to entertain the possibility, *I could be wrong*. In all discussions on all subjects, even on the Bible, I entertain that possibility. Except for one thing, and the apostle Paul said it: "There is one thing I know: Christ and the Crucifixion." I'm willing to discuss and hold up for the possibility of error in everything else that I hold. But I will not hold up for the possibility of error that Jesus Christ is Lord, Savior, the Son of God, and He died on the cross for our sins, and He's resurrected and alive in the world today. That is not up for discussion. Everything else is up for discussion, and I have to be humble enough to say, "Let me hear your point of view. Maybe you can teach me something. Maybe I hold some views that are wrong."

DAN: Jesus came in grace and truth and it seems like we've been doing really well with the truth and not so much with the grace.

TONY: That's such a good verse. When you started that it reminded me of another verse, "Speak the truth in love." I don't see much love out there.

DAN: There seems to be divisiveness for divisiveness' sake.

TONY: And I don't think Jesus would be this way. Anytime Jesus wasn't cool was when He was dealing with bigots. When He went after the Pharisees, "You brood of vipers, you bloodsuckers you . . ." When people were mean Jesus got hard on them.

DAN: Jesus put a priority on relationship; His corrections always come within that context.

TONY: I think we can get too focused on the principle and forget the person.

DAN: We can get hung up on the law when Jesus tried to demonstrate the basics for us: "love God" and "love one another."

DAN: If we demonstrated that love, or as close to that as we can get, what would people outside the faith think?

TONY: There are two stories I want to tell you. Gandhi said, "Everybody in the world understands what Jesus was teaching, except for Christians." Now that's an interesting statement.

DAN: [laughs] It is.

TONY: The other is a quote from Saint Augustine. It's a good quote. "The church is a whore, but she's my mother." You want to talk about unfaithfulness? The church is the unfaithful bride of Christ, but she's also my mother. Without this thing called the church I wouldn't know about Jesus. For all its unfaithfulness, for all its whoring, the church has kept the gospel story alive down through the ages.

Not bad for a first interview, huh? Wow! Campolo amazed me with his candor, understanding, and sincere heart for God. Also, Tony could very likely be the smartest, kindest person I have ever met. You know how sometimes smart people are too busy showing you how smart they are? Tony wasn't like that. He patiently answered my questions, openly shared his perspective and experience. He should serve as tangible proof that a person can have strong opinions on delicate, complicated issues and still be able to engage in a dialogue.

Chapter Four

greetings from
B U T A J E R A

The thing about a journey is, sometimes you can be on one and not even realize it. I've spent the past two years observing the so-called culture wars, interviewed dozens of smart people, and traversed the country dressed up in a hazmat suit plastered with an array of bumper stickers, all in an effort to get people to try and have a conversation about faith and culture in America. In my desperation to escape the escalating monologue of divisive rhetoric, I was determined to find a way to incite understanding and compassionate dialogue. If I had to play the fool in the process, so be it. (And, trust me, it's not much of a leap for me to go from standing start to fool.) This part of my journey has been captured in my feature-length documentary film also entitled *Lord, Save Us From Your Followers*, but, upon further reflection it turns out the journey in question—my journey—began a full year earlier on a trip to Ethiopia.

This trip to the other side of the world came out of the blue sky. A former associate of executive producer Jeff had called ten days earlier to see if we'd be interested in accompanying former U.S. Congressman Tony Hall, now a special United Nations (UN) Ambassador on Global Missions, on his return to Ethiopia for an anniversary of sorts. Tony was one of the first Americans on the ground during the Great Famine. Although he had returned several times, this trip would mark twenty years since his first visit—a visit that had changed him forever.

The invitation, frankly, unsettled me. I had never planned to visit Ethiopia—what with the Communists, famine, plagues, drought, no beaches, I just didn't see the draw. Sorry, I don't mean to sound like a jerk, but this is how I act when I'm afraid. And I was afraid. Jeff was pretty freaked out by the prospect too.

Honestly, I wasn't sure I wanted to go on a trip that would "change me forever." And, hey, we were busy . . . uh . . . doing stuff um . . . important stuff here in Portland. We didn't have time to trot around the globe, for free no less. But, as happens with these things, we felt God moving somewhere in this. We tried to ignore Him, but that never ends well. And when I realized all my objections were fear-based, I tried to talk my mind into believing that there was something to this I just didn't understand yet . . . and the fear must be confronted. Maybe I'd understand later, but staying home because I was afraid of the unknown, afraid of the adventure, or really, afraid of what God might be trying to teach me, would not be acceptable. Amid second thoughts and multiple immunization shots, my cinematographer buddy

Jimmy signed on. He and I had shared many production adventures together, and I was grateful to have an easy-going cowboy like Jimmy at my side for this one. Plus, once Jimmy committed I wouldn't have the nerve to weasel out at the last second.

There were probably thirty of us gathered at the departure gate in the Frankfurt airport: members of the U.S. Agency for International Development (USAID), folks from Tony Hall's office in Rome, and other Americans, who, like us, were invited to see the progress, or lack thereof, brought about by twenty years of relief to Ethiopia. It was exciting to meet our traveling mates and the excitement of our arrival in Ethiopia was building, but there was still a single rogue thought dancing around in the back of my brain.

Food.

I tried to be cool. I tried to suppress this thought, this concern, but as the boarding time grew closer, the thought grew more insistent.

Food?

I casually introduced the topic to Jimmy and Jeff and before long we had worked each other into to a mild frenzy.

Foooooddddd!!!

What would we eat there? Would we be hungry? Would the cooks wash their hands? Would the water they washed their hands with make us sick? Is the food really weird in Ethiopia? Is there any food in Ethiopia? I'm gonna starve, aren't I?

Max, Tony's right-hand man and our key liaison, tried to settle us down by giving us a thorough rundown on the cuisine. Max actually liked Ethiopian food. "It's a little different, a little spicy, but quite delicious," he assured us.

But the more Max talked about the food, the hungrier I became. Besides, Max is one of those super nice guys who never gets thrown off his game and keeps everything in perspective—which is fine, but you don't want someone that easygoing and centered to serve as your Third-World-cuisine restaurant reviewer.

I wanted to eat something now, I recognized. I thought, *If I eat enough now, I can coast for a day or two.* Jimmy, Jeff, and I huddled.

"I saw a McDonald's upstairs," I said.

"Yeah, at the top of the escalator," Jeff seconded.

"I'll take a double cheeseburger and a Coke," said Jim.

"A Quarter Pounder and a chicken sandwich and a Coke," I added.

"I'll go. We have time, right?" asked Jeff.

"We have an hour, and Tony Hall's not even here yet anyway."

Jeff, the intrepid producer, set out in search of our last supper.

"Supersize my fries," Jimmy called after him.

Jimmy and I passed the next fifty-seven minutes visiting with our traveling mates, inching toward the shuttle bus, and waiting expectantly for Jeff to return with our fast food. Finally, when Tony Hall arrived, there were only a couple of us still at the gate. Everyone else had filtered out to the bus. We nodded hello to Tony as Max ushered him out to the last shuttle.

"You guys better come on. This is it," Max insisted.

Jimmy and I looked at each other, then back at the empty escalator. (It totally felt like we were in a movie for a second). *Oh man. We're not even out of the airport, and we have a crisis. Where was my hamburger? Was I going to arrive in Ethiopia already starved? And, incidentally, should we leave Jeff stranded in the Frankfurt airport?* As I started to send Jimmy ahead without me, Jeff appeared at the top of the escalator, smiling, jovial, casual, carrying three big bags of McDonald's fast food. He strode toward us like a hunter who had just bagged a twelve-point deer. (I don't hunt, but I think that's a big one.) Somewhere between my wild arm swinging, Jimmy's scowl, and the fact that we were the only two idiots left at the gate, Jeff's expression changed and his pace quickened. I collected our luggage, and Jimmy waved for the shuttle to wait.

"What the heck happened to you?" I croaked.

"Fast food isn't fast here," Jeff replied. "I just kept waiting and waiting."

We bounded out to the bus. The doors *whooshed* open. Jimmy went for the front door, Jeff and I went to the back door. Just inside the back door stood Tony Hall, a model humanitarian, a politician who uses his position to help others, a kind and gentle man dedicated to serving the poor as God calls us all to do. Jeff saw him and promptly handed me the three steaming bags of McDonald's fast food.

"Here's your food, Dan," he said, a little too loudly. Jeff then veered off and scrambled up the front stairs leaving me standing alone on the tarmac with the burgers and fries. Thanks for that, partner.

I tried to keep a grip on my composure and stepped up onto the bus, scanning for an open seat. There were none, and I had nowhere to hide. The only space was a spot standing next to Tony. I shuffled over next to him, clinging to the same pole for balance.

Running out of options to avoid humiliation, I opted for the direct approach: "Hi, Tony, I'm Dan Merchant." I smiled, trying to ignore the circumstances.

"Hi, Dan. You guys are the film crew, right?"—he smiled—"From Portland?"

"Yes, sir."

"I have good friends in Portland. A beautiful city."

"Yes it is."

By now that magical McDonald's french-fry smell had begun to permeate the crowded shuttle bus. People tried to look away, they tried to ignore the power; but, of course, their olfactory senses were helpless against the golden goodness of the McDonald's fry. I feared that everyone within the immediate blast radius would be saturated by the deep-fry smell. Once it was in their clothes, they'd smell like McDonald's for the whole flight—and they'd probably curse me for the entire trip. I'd be known as French-Fry Guy. Great.

The bus jerked into motion, forcing me to readjust my grip. I tried to balance myself and in the process raised the fry bag to Tony's eye level in what felt like some bizarre fast-food salute. ("Behold, humble subjects! Worship the burgers and fries!")

Tony smiled politely. I was dying. I might as well have taken a french fry out of the bag and shoved it up his nose. There I was squeezed onto a bus full of relief workers, and I was clinging to three bags of American food like it was the last real food I would ever taste. Isn't it funny how your own fear can mock you? The fear initially promises you comfort, but it's a cold comfort . . . it's a trap. Even as the edges of the bags began to tear in my sweaty palms, the burgers and fries were mocking me.

Tony broke the silence, "When I tell people about my visits to Ethiopia, they always say, 'The next time you go on that trip, please call me, I want to go with you.' I always call when I take these trips, but very few of them ever come. They're always busy; they've always got something to do." He looked me square in the eye. "I'm glad you came."

That was a relief. Tony made me feel a little less pathetic. At least I was here, right? Though, I must confess, I greedily chomped on my burgers, fries, and

Coke once I was safely ensconced in my seat on the plane. Tony was gracious not to lambaste me on the bus. I'm sure he'd seen people like me on these trips before. He knew what was in store for me, even if I didn't. He'd seen people cling to their habits, their fears, right up to the moment they were immersed into this other world.

The din in the United Nations-issue Toyota Land Cruiser was overpowering. The vibration off the battered pavement rattled up through the frame, shaking me like a rusted roller coaster in some highly questionable traveling carnival. The wind hissed blinding white noise through the partially lowered windows. Add in the excited commentary from Jimmy and the decibel level was somewhere between a 737 upon take-off and the Who at full throttle in Wembley Stadium. This cranium-rattling sound track was completely at odds with the majestic image of the Great Rift Valley that stretched out in every direction: rolling, grass-covered fields, sweeping gullies climbing and plunging along the muscular landscape, rivers and streams knifing around stands of trees and resolving in long lakes. *Holy cow! This is Ethiopia? I thought this place was supposed to be one big desert of death.*

Our driver, Negussie, a smart, goateed man of fifty or so, told me that we were not far from the Garden of Eden.

"The Garden of Eden? Adam and Eve and the apple and the snake, that Garden of Eden?" I teased.

"Yes. The Great Rift Valley is the cradle of life, where man was born," he smiled as he nodded, seemingly pleased to enlighten me. (The poor, ignorant Westerner who thought he lived in the center of the universe.) I noted the matter-of-fact assurance with which he delivered this news. *Okay, check that off the list. Garden of Eden confirmed.* I asked Negussie if we would have time to find the Ark of the Covenant while we were here.

"That might be more difficult. But follow the Euphrates toward Baghdad; there are those who claim it rests there." Negussie winked. I couldn't tell if he was razzing me or putting an offer on the table.

Jimmy burst out laughing. "The Goose is the man!"

I explained to Negussie that the nickname was a compliment, part of a special language amongst friends. Negussie seemed happy to wear our new moniker, and we had a new best friend, whom I welcomed on this amazing journey.

Now, if you've never been to a third-world country, and I hadn't previous to Ethiopia, it's not going to be like what you think. Even though I'd done my research, I was still blown away because once I was five minutes from the new state-of-the-art airport in Addis Ababa, it was more like traveling to a *time* than traveling to a *place*.

Even the middle-class dwellings in the cities—the ones with a single extension cord supplying power for a VCR or a TV or a toaster—were not much better than the forts crafted in the backyards and vacant lots of America by grade-schoolers playing Huck Finn. But the tin shanties that encircled the more modern elements of the capital soon faded as we bumped down the lonesome, two-lane "paved" road out into the expanse of the Great Rift Valley.

I was starting to feel a strange sensation: with each mile it actually felt like we were physically hurtling back in time. Now, I'm not a history buff, but I'd place most of Ethiopia as dating somewhere around the tenth century. My mind-set was twisted inside out, and I was riding bareback on a total paradigm shift. I mean, I knew a great many here wouldn't have running water or cable television or fancy cars or McDonald's or iPods, but this felt completely alien to me. Where were the power lines? Where were the cars? Where were the traffic lights? Where were the buildings? Where were the neighborhoods? What were those kids doing in that field with a head of cattle and tiny whip? What was that herd of goats doing *in the middle of the road?* Everything would have to be reconsidered. This world wasn't my world minus some frills (okay, minus, all the frills and most of the essentials); it was a different world entirely.

When the universe is stripped completely away, reduced to bare earth and open sky and the unknown, there is room for the real questions to push through to the frontal lobe. Heavy, mind-twisting stuff pressed on me, apparently the questions I had work so hard to ignore. If I really was a Christian, a person who loves God's children, why was it so easy for me to put my own comfort ahead of the needs of others? Why was it so easy for me to donate a little money here and there and get on with my life? Why was it so easy for me to ignore those less fortunate than me? Was Jesus rolling His eyes at me, growing impatient with my lameness? These questions had not occurred to me back in twenty-first-century America, but these questions, and others, were coming fast and furious in tenth-century Ethiopia.

Despite my Internet research prior to this trip, in my mind's eye Ethiopia was frozen in time: specifically, July 13, 1985. My image of Ethiopia was from Live Aid—the unprecedented Bob Geldof organized series of rock concerts broadcast live around the world to raise awareness for those suffering through the great famine. Of all the horrors in the world, this was the tragedy that my favorite rockers of the eighties had come together to support. I was proud of those who participated and had always hoped Live Aid had made a difference. The problems didn't vanish overnight—and twenty years later the country was still precariously perched on the edge—but Live Aid had helped.

I asked Negussie about Live Aid, and though he didn't know the event by name, he knew of the British rock singers who were among the first to take Ethiopia's plight to the world. The Goose quietly referred to this period in Ethiopia's history as "the dark times." Although he alluded to the loss of family members, he quickly skipped over this part of the story to the arrival of relief organizations, the return of the rains, and the cessation of death.

During the course of my week or so in Ethiopia I would probably spend sixty hours riding in the Land Cruiser with the Goose. We became friends (and later e-mail pen pals), but I was only able to get him to share about the dark times for a grand total of about three minutes. I listened intently to the weight of each syllable, looked into the depth of his solemn brown eyes, noted the movement of each deep wrinkle on his face, and gleaned a singular message: *Brother, you don't want to know what I know. Be thankful you have not seen what I have seen.*

I can't really wrap my brain around the circumstances that allowed million upon millions of lives to succumb to famine, disease, and an absurd border war in 1984 and 1985. I don't have a reference point for that scale of suffering, because it is, mercifully, beyond my comprehension.

Later in the week Tony Hall would tell me of his first morning in Ethiopia. Tony was among the first Westerners allowed into the country by the Marxist government who, inexplicably, denied aid workers access to Ethiopia even as the famine's devastating effects were taking their toll.

Even twenty years later, there was sadness in his eyes and a dry, matter-of-fact quality to his voice as Tony described that day.

"I went to a place up-country, and there were just thousands of people who were in trouble. I'd never seen anything like that. One of the compounds that I went to was the Sisters of Charity. A doctor and a sister met me there, and he told me that a lot of people had come overnight. And there were thousands surrounding the compound wanting to get in and get help.

"The doctor said to me, 'I have to go out and pick five, six, seven children; that's all we can handle.' And there are thousands out there." Tony waved a hand as if to paint a picture of despair stretching out from his feet all the way to the horizon.

Tony cleared his throat and continued, "The doctor said, 'I want you to see this.' So I went out with him. As I was walking out among the people they would hold up their babies. They were thinking that maybe I was a doctor. You could tell they were saying, 'Take my baby. Take my baby.' Because they knew if we didn't take them, if we didn't select them, they were probably not going to make it that day. And many probably didn't."

Tony looked off into the distance or maybe off into the past from the balcony of the Sheraton Hotel in Addis Ababa where we were talking. I waited quietly for him to continue.

"After that I went farther up-country to a plateau and saw maybe fifty-thousand people who had walked sixty, seventy, and some had walked for almost one hundred kilometers. These people had heard that there was going to be food." Tony's gaze shifted directly to me, as if to ask, *Is that not the saddest thing you've ever heard?* I tried to imagine what these poor people must've felt in that moment when they realized they had not arrived at an oasis, but at a graveyard.

Tony shifted his weight. "This drought was absolutely wiping out all these farmers. So they were moving to this place in hopes of getting blankets and food and water—but nobody was there. So after walking, after selling everything they had to get to this place, they just kind of laid down"—he swallowed hard—"and they moaned and they died."

I didn't know what to say. I just listened to Tony, unable to grasp his story.

"And I walked among them," Tony continued. "And I saw, I don't know how many children I saw die in a very short time, but maybe twenty-five or twenty-eight children in a half-hour, an hour. It was incredible. And that was the first experience I had here in 1984."

"What do you do with that?" I asked. "How does seeing something like that change you?"

He nodded. This was a question Tony Hall had answered many times in the past twenty years. "It was one of those situations, if you've never seen it before you are staggered by it. Going home on the plane to America after that week I spent in Ethiopia, I decided that this was what I was going to focus on. I was going to focus on poverty. I was going to focus on hunger, both in the world and in my own country. That changed my life, that day up-country in Ethiopia."

"How are things different between 1984 and today? Are things improving or are we just running around in circles?" I asked.

"Things are better. In 1984 we had a million people die; last year they had a very bad drought here and thousands of people died, but it wasn't a million, so that has changed. The government has changed; the government here is much better now. The government in those days was communist. They had a drought and famine here for six months before they let anybody into the country even to know about what was going on. Then the BBC came in, and they were able to film what was going on. Then pressure was put on this government to let people in here to help. By the time we got in here, a million people had died. Last year when we had a serious, serious problem in this country, the government let the world know. They invited everybody in, they pre-positioned food all over the country in advance of the drought, and they did a lot of good things. Do they need a lot of changes in this country? Absolutely. But the difference between today and 1984? Much better."

Fortunately, things had changed in Ethiopia between Tony's first day and my first day. During my week, I'd learn about the web of non-governmental organizations (NGOs) propping up the citizenry with education, improved farming techniques, early drought warning, and generous donations of seed and grain from the world's wealthiest countries.

Somewhat surprisingly, the population of Ethiopia has actually grown from thirty-five million to around seventy million since 1984. But with only three million people living in the cities, this is still a society on the edge. We're talking about sixty-seven million people living in very difficult, rural conditions, hamstrung by primitive farming techniques, surviving on the food they can grow for themselves, and ultimately relying on the precarious timing of rainfall for life.

Jimmy and I got used to bouncing around inside the Toyota after the second hour. My head banged off the ceiling no less than a dozen times, but I settled into my groove right about the time the mild concussion set in.

The caravan of matching United Nations 4x4s had come to a stop at a filling station about an hour from our destination at a feeding station near Butajera. I stepped out of the vehicle to stretch my legs and take a look around. The pavement directly around the cars seemed familiar: cars, gas pumps, and small building. But the muddy street seemed to be a dividing line between modern times and the Middle Ages. A horribly disfigured elderly man with some kind of growth on his neck that was probably the size of a football paddled around on a small cart. In our culture, such a malady would be operated on. But this man, who was probably sixty or seventy, had lived his whole life with it. It was difficult to see things so out of the ordinary and yet to react would be out of the ordinary in this place.

I leaned back on our truck and chatted through the window with Negussie and Jimmy. Even though my mouth kept moving, I was soaking in this strange land, pretending to be unfazed. I can't quite remember how we got on the subject, but I do remember telling Negussie that I was a Christian. He thought it was interesting that I had actually been baptized in a river as a teenager. I didn't think much of it at the time, but later in the day Tony Hall pulled me aside.

"I wanted to mention to you that we refer to ourselves as a 'Follower of Jesus,' rather than a 'Christian,'" he said gently.

Follower of Jesus? From the expression on his face, Tony had heard this conversation before. I was forty-one years old, and I still felt like a rookie. Clearly, my loud "I have a thought about that" tone of voice had carried farther than I thought at the gas station earlier today.

"You see, over here, *Christian* comes with a lot of baggage, a lot of meaning attached to it that distracts from Jesus," he continued.

"What, like the Crusades?" I asked.

"In this culture a thousand years ago feels just like yesterday. The Crusades mean something different to a population that's half Muslim."

"I'm sorry, I didn't think about that," I said.

"We're trying to see good work done here like Jesus would do—so we don't want to distract people or disrupt relationships," he said.

"Okay, Follower of Jesus it is," I smiled.

I admit to being a little embarrassed because I had been trying so hard not to be a clod-footed American stomping around in someone else's country. I was afraid I had upset the Goose and he had complained, but it turned out I hadn't offended Negussie. Someone had overheard my booming voice and wanted to get me on the same page as the rest of the delegation.

Later, after I thought more about it, of course, Follower of Jesus makes sense. The term is apolitical, even "Follower of Christ" has "Christ" in the title which, I suppose, could lead to an argument about Jesus versus Mohammed. And when you're in a land where half the people are Muslim and half are Christian and they're getting along together just fine, I see Tony's point about not distracting from the work at hand. This posture clearly demonstrated to me that these Followers of Jesus are here to meet a need and not win an argument.

A couple of days later Tony Hall showed us an amazing oasis called Project Mercy. This project is nestled in the foothills, below the highlands of central Ethiopia, about three kilometers from a small town called Butajera (maybe eighty kilometers southeast from Addis Ababa). Project Mercy stands as a promise for the future. The education that six hundred children are receiving will transform this country as surely as the physical complex of Project Mercy has transformed this village of straw huts. Tony described Project Mercy as the most complete independent project he'd ever seen: classrooms, guest quarters for dozens of orphans and teachers, kitchens, food storage warehouses, drip irrigation gardens, livestock pens, a metal shop, and the only hospital for sixty kilometers.

Project Mercy was founded in the mid-90s by Demeke Tekle-Wold and his wife Marta Gabre Tsadick, Ethiopia's first female senator. She was in

office when the Communists overthrew the government in the late 1970s. Marta and her family fled for their lives. After the dark times, Marta and Demeke were able to return to their homeland and realize the vision of restoring what drought and famine had destroyed.

Marta tells all, "Faith built this place. We were obedient, but we did not do this, faith built this place." To tell their story properly would require an entire book, but suffice it to say everyone at Project Mercy respectfully referred to Marta and Demeke as Mother and Father. I never met Mother Teresa of Calcutta , but I'll bet you she and Marta would've been friends. The loving leadership provided by this woman was completely infectious. But that's the way most of the people I met in Ethiopia were: unbelievably gracious, joyous, open, warm, funny, and delightful. Suffice it to say, this did not compute. Happy people? In this place? This made no sense to me. And, just to clarify, this countenance was not a blissful ignorance or some disconnect from reality; it seemed to be some kind of ability to endure suffering with grace and reap the lessons and even growth from hardship. Weird, right?

I spoke with a few teens at Project Mercy about faith—which was optional, by the way, though the vast majority of the kids ended up exploring this faith that had called Demeke and Marta home from America.

One teen told me, "We are brothers. Your mother is not my mother and your skin is white and my skin is black, but we are brothers because we love Jesus. We are brothers in Christ. In heaven, these differences will not matter. We are brothers now, and we will be brothers in heaven." This young man brushed his teeth with his finger this morning and yet he saw the truth with stunning clarity.

Another kid who had lost both his parents to AIDS told me, "My mother she die, not for me. My father he die, but not for me. Jesus, He died for me. I have life because Jesus died for me."

I remember thinking, *Wow. They're talking like they really believe this stuff. Profound.* When they talked to me about their faith, I saw it so purely, so cleanly, I almost didn't recognize it. Their reliance on God was so complete, their belief so tangible, I was taken aback.

That night we were treated to a special banquet and were told there would be a special musical performance.

After dinner the choir entered quietly, but their excitement was felt nevertheless. The first row shuffled into place. These were the youngest—mostly girls but a few boys mixed in. I placed the youngest at age four or five. Their bodies were well-trained and still, but their eyes danced around the room, intrigued by the audience of white faces. The second row slipped into place; this group must have been junior-high age, twelve to fifteen maybe. Then finally, the leaders who comprised the third row: the high-school-aged kids in their mid-to late teens. The older kids were more stoic, perhaps more focused on performing well for this group of foreign friends and dignitaries.

I sat in the back, behind the rows of banquet tables, away from the important folks who could wield influence and bring support to Project Mercy.

After a few words from Marta, who specifically welcomed an important politician visiting from the Capitol, and a brief introduction from the choir director, the children began to sing. All told there were maybe twenty-five or thirty children, but I was startled by their power, volume, and precision—as a choir they were one voice. They were singing in their native tongue, Amharic I think (hey, I did pick up a few syllables in my time there), so I had no idea what they were singing about.

I studied the face of each singer—bright eyes, open hearts—and I began to feel a little disoriented. I was absolutely enchanted by the passion in their voices, by the gorgeous melody, and . . . by something else. I felt my own heart swell, my skin began to tingle, and I noticed the hair on my arms literally stood on end. I glanced quickly around the room and saw that all conversation had ceased—even the important folks were transfixed by the choir, looking on with a combination of fascination and awe.

As the song circled back to the chorus, I felt a hot tear run down my cheek. I focused on the smallest child, a little boy of five or so, wearing a loose-fitting, long shirt. And this kid was just singing his guts out, rising up on his toes as he articulated the chorus. As the choir hit the chorus full on, I had this strange sensation, as if the top of my head had opened up. The tears were flowing from both eyes now. I was fully emotionally reacting, but to what? Sure the kids were cute and the song was pretty, but something else was going on. I took a deep breath and relaxed. The singing continued to fuel this odd feeling of peace, of euphoria—and then I understood: we were no longer alone.

This may be a little early in the journey to get "woo-woo" on you, but I'm here to tell you, the Holy Ghost had walked into that meeting room in the middle of Africa. Actually, it felt as if the Holy Ghost had come in, taken a chicken wing from the buffet, sat down, put His feet up on the table, and started to direct the choir. Heck, it sounded as if the Holy Spirit was singing along with them. I'm telling you, God had never felt more real to me than in that moment. I could feel Him nudging me with an elbow, "Hey, aren't these kids great? Man, I love kids."

I'm telling you, this feeling of knowing that God is *everywhere*, the idea He would come and share in the beauty of this moment, that He would make such beauty possible was so wonderful.

The children sang as if they truly knew Him. Their belief and passion were so inspiring to me. *Passion*, there's the word isn't it? Faith in America, Christianity in America, seems to have become about the argument, the persuasion, a justification of beliefs. I wish every Christian and atheist could've sat in that banquet room along with God and enjoyed this children's choir. If *us* and *them* could've sat together while those kids sang, the conversation would've changed from "You're wrong about this and that!" to "Ain't it beautiful?"

The choir performed three more songs. I sat quietly in the back, occasionally wiping the tears from my face. When the children concluded their performance, they filed out as quietly as they had entered and conversation returned
to the room. My emotions ebbed; I wiped my eyes and cleared my throat.
Jimmy, who had been filming from across the room caught my eye. I just smiled
and shrugged, not feeling any burden to explain or elaborate on the moment.

As I settled down, I did get curious about something; I wondered about
the lyrics of the first song. What were they singing about in their mysterious
tongue? I found the choir director, thanked him for his work with the children, and inquired about the chorus of that first song. "Jesus Will Carry Me
Through the Fire," he said, smiling. Well, doesn't that just figure, a gospel
song, but of course. Apparently, my heart had understood the song even
though my head couldn't decipher the words. Clearly, the Holy Spirit heard
the song and, interpreting it as an invitation, dropped in for a visit. That
may sound crazy, but that's what happened.

I know this kind of thing can happen anywhere at anytime, but it rarely
does. I suppose it occasionally happens at some rocking, hand-waving
church that invites the Holy Spirit and actually expects Him to show up. I
guess when you believe, and when you're looking, you see Him everywhere—even in the oddest, smallest, most insignificant places. But when we
don't look, when we're not open, we don't see Him. That doesn't mean He's
not there. Pretty weird, but I love it. God isn't a set of beliefs, He isn't some
kind of oath we take. He's the one who created this place we dwell in, and
He's willing to interact with us if we're open to Him.

My friends from Ethiopia actually believe all the lines we say in church
all the time. You know: "Lord fill me up with Your loving-kindness," or
"Lord, let me be a vessel of Your love." Those dear people in Africa reminded
me *this is real!* And by real I mean, it's real like my left foot is real.

When you understand that Jesus' love is sufficient, when you actually get
that God loves you, this is how you sound when you sing. When you actually
believe God has a plan for you, even if the road is hard, there is a peace that
you carry. *These guys act as if they believe this stuff* . . . and if I'm not acting this
way, then what do I really believe? When you see this you ask yourself some
questions, things like: *Are they nuts?* No, wait, they believe what I say I believe.
Am I nuts? I sure don't act as if I believe this. A*m I happy because I understand*

that God loves me? Am I happy because I've been validated by people or my career accomplishments? Am I happy because I have a nice wife and two kids and two cars? Am I happy? Who am I?

It may seem funny to you that I didn't immediately realize this was the beginning of my journey. I mean, it was a physical journey. I did literally fly across the globe, plop down into a four-wheel-drive Toyota with a wizened guide, and proceeded directly to the edge of my reality. Sure, it's obvious now, but at the time I needed to be unplugged from my daily distractions in order even to create enough space to contemplate how others were living. I needed to be transplanted back to the tenth century in order to get a little perspective.

There's an old line that goes, "When you see the way things are, you can't pretend you're blind."

Chapter Five

al
F R A N K E N

I didn't know Al Franken grew up near Minneapolis, Minnesota. I had always associated the Twin Cities with the '80s music scene that brought the world-trailblazing artists from Prince to the Replacements. In my mind Al Franken was a New York City guy, which, incidentally, is where he was born. I suppose my Big Apple image formed because he was a seminal member of the one-show comedy revolution known as *Saturday Night Live*. Al and his comedic partner, Tom Davis, were instrumental writers and producers during the groundbreaking heydays of *SNL*, and at the dawn of the '80s, Al cemented his importance to pop culture by proclaiming the new decade "The Al Franken Decade."

Even from the early days of *SNL* I was aware of Franken, and he always seemed smart to me. The glasses and sport jacket made him seem like a grown-up big-city intellectual, and the deadpan, "I'm not trying to perform," delivery style re-inforced my perception that some producer let the crazy-genius writer on the air by mistake. I guess I also remember hearing he was a Harvard man which, to an eleven-year-old, meant two things: everybody who went there was a smarty-pants and Southern Cal's football team would kill the Harvard team.

As a young teen, I enjoyed Franken's anarchic, socially relevant comedy because I sensed intelligence behind the silliness, and I felt that Franken respected the audience. When Al went on the air and bashed embattled NBC President Fred Silverman (responsible for timeless classics like *Manimal* and *Misfits of Science*) because he had a limo and Franken didn't, there was demand for justice at the heart of the absurd "A Limo for a Lame-O" bit.

I followed Franken into his post-*SNL* years, and the success of his self-help addicted character Stuart Smalley: "I'm good enough, I'm smart enough and, doggone it, people like me," which spawned a book and major motion picture. In fact, to this day, rival Bill O'Reilly spitefully (or perhaps comically) refers to Franken as Stuart Smalley, never uttering Al's real name. Bill has to be doing schtick, too, right? I wonder if they get a beer together after work.

Later Franken surfaced on *Comedy Central* doing satiric, often biting, political commentary during election season, before graduating to full-on political commentator status with his best-selling books including, *Rush Limbaugh Is a Big Fat Idiot, The Truth (with jokes)*, and *Lies and the Lying Liars Who Tell Them: A Fair and Balanced Look at the Right*. In 2004, he began hosting *The Al Franken Show*, the flagship program on the new progressive (read liberal) radio network, Air America.

While I pride myself on being somewhat apolitical, Al Franken and I share different views on many subjects. I've always appreciated his ability to make me laugh even while I'm disagreeing . . . and when we're sharing that laugh, I'm reminded that the differences may not be as big as I think. Also, for me, Franken's self-deprecating, dry comedy invites all of us to look at our foibles . . . and we all have them.

But Al Franken's dramatically distinguished himself from the pundit pack with one simple act: he accepted my invitation to be interviewed for *Lord, Save Us From Your Followers*. He was willing to have the conversation when others were asking, "Who is in your movie so far?" Plus Franken's proximity to the culture wars made him an attractive interview. As a champion for the

Left, Al regularly clashes with Bill O'Reilly, Ann Coulter, Rush Limbaugh, and other stalwarts of the Right. I wanted to understand more about *us* versus *them*, and this key player in the media circus was willing to talk.

∝

On a wet and warm day in April 2006, Jimmy and I were rolling anvil cases of video equipment down Second Avenue in Minneapolis and into a main floor conference room in the building where Al broadcast *The Al Franken Show*.

An hour later, Al Franken appeared, on time, wearing a blue oxford, navy blue jacket, khaki's, and white sneakers, and humming an old Johnny Cash tune—a tune that Jimmy began to sing. Now the fact Jimmy began to sing along with Al is significant because just moments before Al arrived I had given Jimmy my, "I'm the director, let me do the talking" speech. But, you have to understand his magical, easy-goin' Wichita way of connecting with people that defies nature. It is not uncommon for me to hear Jimmy say something that makes me cringe and should shock and offend, but instead, miraculously, supernaturally, he's made a new friend. Understanding this amazing phenomenon that surrounds Jimmy rarely prevents me from giving him a nervous, pre-interview "Let me do the talking" speech. I guess it's just a dance we do.

So, appropriately humbled again, I sat quietly until Al and Jimmy finished their duet, which, for two rumbling baritones, sounded pretty nice.

Al smiled, studied me for a second. "So what's this for again?"

What's this for? You have to love a guy who will show up for an interview just because someone asked. My executive producer, Jeff, said it was because Air America was hurting for ratings (they were), but I'm sticking with "Al's a decent guy even if he is a liberal."

I explained to Al my whole "Why is the gospel of love dividing America?" journey. Al nodded. I saw interest and understanding in his eyes, familiar territory to him no doubt.

DAN: I was fascinated and confused to see that a conference was held last month in Washington, DC, called "A War on Christians." What do you make of that?

AL: I suppose there is a war on Christians . . . in Sudan, and China, and evidently Afghanistan. I mean, there is actually, but there's not one in the United States. And it just cracks me up.

DAN: Last Christmas we heard a lot of noise about a War on Christmas, earlier today we were over at the St. Paul City Hall where the Easter Bunny was ejected—

AL: I've never seen anything like this. This is really silly. There's no war on Christians. There may be Christians who think this is a Christian country, when our constitution is very, very clear.

Al exploded with laughter—something he does quite regularly and loudly. There is something I trust about a person who is so comfortable owning such a boisterous laugh. Having myself been teased for decades about my own explosive, synapse-disrupting laughter, I find yet another thing in common with this liberal, secular Jew from the Midwest.

DAN: Religious liberty and Christian country are two different things?

AL: They're the actual opposite. The whole point is that there is no established religion. The government can't establish religion. And they think that they're not allowed to practice their faith by not doing prayers in school. You can pray silently to yourself in school and kids do, I'm sure, all the time before exams. But a public school can't sanction "a prayer" because that's been ruled to violate the establishment clause. You know, I'd be perfectly happy to have school prayer in the country if it were the Shema.

Al laughed again, then paused, waiting for some kind of recognition from me. Meanwhile, my brain was swimming. The Shema? Okay, I guess I'm supposed to know this prayer, clearly a Hebrew prayer—another embarrassing example of how we Christians don't bother to know anything about beliefs that aren't held by us. This is particularly embarrassing considering half of our Bible is the Jewish Scriptures (more than half really, if you count pages), and, yeah, Jesus was a Jew too. A couple of significant connections between Christians and Jews. So forgive me if I felt a little lame that I had no idea what Al Franken was talking about.

AL: You know, "Shema Yisarael Adonai Eloheinu, Adonai echad."

Okay, I'm sure that was Hebrew, or wait, is it Yiddish? After a beat, Al responded to my blank stare with the English translation.

AL: "Hear O Israel, the Lord our God, the Lord is One." Fine. You want prayer in school that'll be it. But you don't do that."

That is a nice prayer, I thought to myself, and Franken's point made great sense: who gets to choose the prayer? Why shouldn't Al get to choose? He's just as American as I am. Why does Judge Roy Moore think he should choose the prayer? Forget him, I want to choose it, and I pick, "God is great, God is good, let us thank Him for our food; by His hand, we are fed, thank You for this daily bread. Amen." That prayer has been stuck in my head since I was five years old; might as well put it to some good use, right? Plus it's an easy one for kids to say. Okay, maybe it's not perfect for starting the school day, but it's a good prayer, and I say we're going with that one.

See? You're already thinking of the prayer you'd prefer, right?

What about a community where a class is comprised of mostly Hispanic Catholic children? Should they pray the Nicene Creed in Spanish while the Baptist kids stand around awkwardly looking at each other? I'm starting to understand the dexterity required in fully embracing the religious liberty concept: all of the various religions and denominations have the freedom to worship as they wish, without being dictated to by anyone.

Al snapped my reverie by launching into an anecdote from his school days that further illustrated his position on prayer in school.

AL: I went to a school that was chartered at the turn of the century, a school here in Minneapolis for Protestant boys. They started letting Jews in during the 1950s to keep the SAT scores up, frankly. So that's how I got in. [Al peers over the top of his glasses with a grin that says, "I'm kidding . . . but not really."]

They had chapel in the morning, and you had to wear a jacket and tie, and I actually liked chapel. I liked everybody getting together in one place for announcements. There were Protestant hymns, and every junior and senior had to speak at least once. It was a great way to wake up. Tom Davis and I started performing in chapel doing announcements for other groups. I loved chapel. But when the Protestant hymns came I wouldn't sing them because I'm Jewish.

One day my math teacher stops me, "Mr. Franken, I want you to stay back."

I go, "Okay, sure."

And he says, "I notice in chapel you don't sing the hymns."

Al laughed and recreated a look that was part trepidation and part shock.

> AL: I remember going "Whoa," because I immediately know what this is. I respond, "Yeah, well, I'm Jewish and um, uh, since they're sacred I don't think I should undermine that in any way by singing something I don't believe in."
>
> The teacher said, "You want to get into a good college don't you?"
>
> "Yeah . . ."
>
> "And to get into college you need good math grades?"
>
> "Right . . ."
>
> The teacher pats me on the shoulder, "I'd sing the hymns."
>
> So the next day I sang, "Onward Christian soldiers marching as to war . . ."

Al sat up straight in the interview chair, arms swinging with military precision as he belted out one of the most well-known hymns in history with a passion that would bring a tear to Pat Robertson's eyes. I almost fell out of my chair laughing.

> AL: And I was a resilient kid. It didn't mean anything to me; I just thought it was funny. And sometimes I would substitute *Moses* for *Jesus* as I sang. But that was a private school, and they can do what they want. I could've taken this to the headmaster and said, "That's wrong," but it's their school. But in a public school you

can't do that. You can't have kids saying anything that might make them uncomfortable; you can't require a kid to do a prayer. And that doesn't mean you're stopping people from observing their religion, it means you're not establishing a religion. I'm almost describing something that seems too basic to me that I shouldn't have to.

A couple of months later, I would interview radio talk-show host Michael Reagan, who as a conservative evangelical Christian is at the other end of the political spectrum from Al Franken. But Reagan, the adopted son of the late President Ronald Reagan, had a take on this topic Franken would've found compelling. Reagan said, "Why are we asking the state to decide on a prayer for our kids? We should be praying with our kids *before* they go to school. How many of us are doing that? I don't want the state to have that job."

Al Franken and I continued our conversation, exploring the obvious and increasingly noisy divide between Left and Right, between red state and blue state, between Christian and nonbeliever.

AL: I used to go to Christian Coalition events quite often to try and find out what the other people were talking about. And I like the people at Christian Coalition events; 90 percent of them are really nice people. They're actually very concerned about things you should be concerned about, the coarsening of our culture and so on. Now some people would think from some of the stuff I've done I'm responsible for some coarsening from *Saturday Night Live;* I don't think so. I think there's some horrible stuff in our culture, too, but I get offended by banality. I get offended by half the commercials on TV, so that's taste. But I'd say that the people at Christian Coalition events are nicer than the people at the Democratic Convention, by and large. But there is this 10 percent that are just kinda . . .

Al's hands gestured uncertainly as he struggled to find just the right words. I think he wanted to say "kinda crazy," but instead showed admirable restraint.

AL: They're kinda, kinda, not nice and kinda hostile and kinda angry about this whole thing. And I would get in conversations with people on this kind of subject, and they knew who I was, kind of. "What are you doing here?" they'd ask.

But I'd get in a conversation circle and say, "I'll tell you why I don't believe in school prayer," and I'd say the thing about the Shema, and say, "As a Jew, I don't believe that Jesus was the Son of God. I just don't believe that."

And I remember a guy going to me, "So you're calling Jesus a liar?"

I said, "Uh, no, I don't think so."

He said, "Well Jesus says, 'When you look upon Me you look upon the Father.' So you're calling Jesus a liar. You're saying He isn't God."

And I said, "Okay . . . maybe it was a misquote. That could happen, that happens. Maybe Jesus said it, and He thought He was God and maybe He's just a little woo-woo," which the other people knew was a joke [Al explodes with laughter].

And then I said, "Or maybe what Jesus meant was that when you look upon anyone you look upon the Father, that there's God in all of us; maybe that's what He meant."

The other nine people all went "aaaahhhh, that's really nice." And he just hated it, and just went like, I think he actually said, "No one ever accused you Jews of not being clever." [Al throws his arms up in the air, laughing again.]

I went, "Okay, you and I should probably just agree to disagree on things, and I'll talk to the other folks."

And it's that one-tenth of that group that ends up leading or influencing some of the others. I don't think they're well motivated.

DAN: Is it this 10 percent that have the microphone right now? Talking about motivation, there are cases of people playing the "God card" as a shield or using it to distract.

AL: All the time. The God card is used all the time. I don't understand. Especially on things like poverty. Cutting taxes for the rich so you can cut programs for the poor—it just seems so obviously anti-thetical to what Jesus preached.

Al, who tended to retreat into a slouch as he talked, suddenly sat up and something about his expression told me a joke was coming.

AL: As I often say, "If you cut out every passage in the New Testament where Jesus talks about helping the least among us, helping the poor, if you literally cut every one of those out with scissors, you'd have a perfect box for smuggling Rush Limbaugh's drugs in." You have to go to Jesus' original intent.

Yeah, okay, that's funny and makes a point, but also illustrates why there are plenty of people who get down on Al for taking cheap shots. His "Who, me?" look got a laugh from me.

DAN: There are two-thousand-something verses about taking care of the poor and loving one another—the stuff you can't get an argument from anybody on, because there is good intention there.

AL: You gotta interpret that stuff with a strict interpretation there. "It's easier for a camel to get through the eye of a needle than it is for a rich man to get into heaven." But now it's "If you're rich it must mean that you are good. You are rich because you deserve it, because God loves you." It's totally flipped. There is this Gospel of Wealth that says if you become rich it's because God has smiled on you and you're a good person. The people who are bad are the poor people, because they aren't rugged individuals and they're lazy and it's their fault.

I'm reminded of a cartoon called "The Gospel of Supply Side Jesus" in Al's book *Lies and the Lying Liars Who Tell Them*. Supply Side Jesus warns His disciples not to feed the lepers because that would only encourage people to become lepers: if they knew there was free food involved, it would give them incentive not to avoid leprosy.

Hey, nobody said comedy was pretty. But again, as believers who claim to follow the Bible, it is confusing to outsiders how we can be selective in the biblical truths we choose to emphasize.

Al and I concluded our interview by hitting several of the hot-button issues that seem to be central to the culture wars. Certainly, these complicated issues are the ones that get the most play in the media and have been used extensively by various groups as political wedge issues and issues to mobilize a voting block.

DAN: What about intelligent design?

AL: I think intelligent design is creationism in a tuxedo. There's no doubt that the motive behind it is to sneak creationism in. If you stated my view of God it would be very close to what the intelligent design people are saying: "The world is so amazing and complex and great—there must be something behind it." And I also believe in evolution. I think we should teach science in the science class and teach religion and philosophy in religion and philosophy class. We really have to be careful in our society to value science.

The stupid thing is when they say, "It's just the theory of evolution, so it's just a theory." Well, in science a theory is an overarching explanation of something that can actually be shown by experimentation. There's the theory of gravity.

Al kindly demonstrated the theory of gravity by suspending his coffee cup above the conference table. "I have a feeling this cup will fall." He grinned. The cup dropped, coffee sloshed out. Al laughed hard. "There ya go! And it does it every single time." He picked up the cup and dropped it again. "See? Amazing. So I'd say the theory of gravity has been pretty well established." He shrugged and stared dramatically. "So is the theory of evolution."

I'll grant Franken his larger point: there was little question that the intelligent design folks were dressing up creationism rather than truly playing in the "science sandbox." This position spawned the existence of the satiric alternative to Yahweh—the Flying Spaghetti Monster. When the school board ruckus in Dover, Pennsylvania, was in full splendor over the addition of the intelligent design curriculum to the science classes, an engineer decided to accept the scientific argument put forth by the ID folks: the world is too complicated, too amazing, too intricate, and too non-accidental, so it must've been designed by an intelligent force. "Fine," said this engineer, "it was designed by an intelligent force—the Flying Spaghetti Monster from Outer Space. He designed the universe . . . and I have as much proof the FSM is behind all this as you do that the God of Abraham is behind this." If you want to argue science, you have to argue by science's rules. It's completely fair to say, "I *believe* the words in this Bible, I *believe* God made all we see. But, of course, I can't prove it." Science is a prove-it game, so if evolution makes you unhappy, defeat it scientifically.

DAN: Let's talk about the upset regarding the separation of church and state.

AL: I really am a firm believer of church and state and think it's a good thing for religion. We're the most religious developed country in the world, I believe, and I think one of the reasons is that we have a healthy separation of church and state. And because of that religion has flourished in our country. It's a good thing for religion. So I think, for example, that "under God" probably shouldn't be in the Pledge of Allegiance; it wasn't put in there until the 1950s, but it's not that big a deal to me.

"In God We Trust" probably shouldn't be on the coins—I don't care. It's a real fine line; in France they don't let Muslim girls cover their heads—that's ridiculous. They say that violates the separation of church and state in France. They don't let Muslim kids cover their heads with traditional Islamic clothing? That seems wrong to me. Now it's the same logic, I guess, that I apply to certain things. I don't think you should have the Ten Commandments up in the schools. If someone did that I wouldn't make a big deal out of it. But if it goes to a judge the judge would have to say, "Yeah, you gotta take it down."

Agree or disagree, Al's tone suggested a reasonability, room for compromise of the kind that makes our democracy possible. "I think we gotta calm down . . . and focus on important things." Al laughed his crazy laugh.

DAN: What about one of the stickier issues like the Federal Marriage Amendment? This states marriage is reserved for a man and a woman.

AL: I just think that's wrong. I'm probably in the minority on this issue, but I think it'll move to a majority. I believe in equal rights in marriage. Forty years ago there were states where people thought interracial couples shouldn't marry. I think 98 percent of Americans are kinda embarrassed that existed forty years ago. I think forty years from now, 90 percent of Americans will be embarrassed we didn't allow gay people to marry. The threat to marriage is adultery and divorce. [Al shrugged and paused for effect.] "That's the threat to families." [His eyes twinkled, he sat up again—I felt another comedy bit coming on.] I said to Newt Gingrich the other day, "Don't you want for a gay couple what you had with your first wife? Don't you want for a gay couple what comes with that bond of fidelity that you had with your second wife? Don't you want for that gay couple what comes with that lifelong commitment that you may or may not have with your third wife?" I have no idea what's going on there, I have no idea what the hell is going on there.

I cringed as I laughed. Again, a fair point, at the expense of Newt, albeit, but we Christians really ought to keep our sanctimony in check when talking about marriage when the divorce rate for believers is running on par with everyone else. Al's bombastic laugh subsided.

AL: Hey listen, sometimes people get married three times. I don't want to be judgmental; it's good that people get divorced sometimes. But, for goodness sakes, don't you want people to be married? Don't you want people to be devoted to each other? And don't you want equal rights for people? I think Tony Campolo has this idea, which is maybe a good idea, that the state marries people in civil ceremonies and they're observed by the state as married, the same as a civil union. And if churches want to marry people they can marry.

For some reason people expect because I'm in show business,

sort of in show business, I'm barely in show business . . . I don't know what they think, but when I'm introduced to speak somewhere it will go, "Mr. Franken now lives in Minneapolis, he's written best sellers, he has two children, and has been married for thirty years." The crowd erupts in applause and I go, "What?"

[Al impersonates the shocked response of a crowd member.] "Married for thirty years? And in show business?" [Al laughs heartily.] It's just fear everybody . . . fear of being alone. It's no big achievement, I'm afraid. [He laughs again.]

Al and I talked for a few minutes about a possible run for the Minnesota senate seat held by Norm Coleman—at this meeting he was noncommittal but offered: "I'm preparing myself in case I decide to." A few months later, Franken did indeed declare his candidacy and, as of this writing, is campaigning around the state to gain support for the Democratic Party nomination.

We closed our time talking about comedy.

DAN: Comedy seems to have this way of illuminating and getting people to let their guard down. I think people are more open to consider what you have to say because you do it with humor.

AL: I hope so, that's the point. It's also to make it more fun to read. I try to make what I call "nutritional candy." You can eat what I produce because it's good for you, but it's also fun to eat. I make candy bars that are good for you.

Al exploded one last time with that wonderful laugh.

As Jimmy and I packed up the gear, I felt great. Not only because Al Franken turned out to be a good interview and a generous conversationalist, but because I learned, again, that it's possible to have a lively, enlightening give-and-take with someone who doesn't necessarily agree with you on every topic. I learned things from Al, and I hope Al learned things from me.

I guess I was feeling good because that's how it feels to be part of a dialogue. It's a lot more fun than being part of a debate, that's for sure.

Chapter Six

stand and
D E L I V E R

I had followed the career of Senator Rick Santorum for many years. A Republican from Pennsylvania, he was elected to the Senate in 1994 and quickly became a visible, unapologetic spokesman for conservative causes that became important to the evangelical community. Santorum, who comes from a Catholic upbringing, was well-known for being outspoken on the volatile issues of abortion, same-sex-marriage, and the intelligent design versus evolution. Rick Santorum's strong moral stance engendered him to the Religious Right. He appeared at events featuring Dr. James Dobson, Tony Perkins, and Dr. Jerry Falwell and became *persona non grata* with his counterparts on the Left. I found Santorum particularly interesting because his boyish looks, sturdy, soft-spoken nature, and no-nonsense embodiment of family values seemed so American—and yet he was vilified as a "hate monger." I found this curious because, despite sharing the stage with old guard of the Religious Right at Justice Sunday III, Santorum was very matter-of-fact in expressing what he thought was right and what was wrong. As far as I could see, he refrained from blatant hyperbole and was fair about his arguments. You could disagree with his positions, but they didn't strike me as unfair positions.

Another thing I found fascinating, especially for a politician, was that Santorum steadfastly represented his beliefs even as his popularity slipped. He clearly believed the values he was standing up for, as opposed to being a rider on the "values voters" train. As the 2006 midterm elections approached, the tide had turned against what Santorum's adversaries termed "wedge politics" and, like many Republicans, Santorum was voted out of office.

I interviewed Rick in early December following the elections and found him to be a humble, thoughtful, and pleasant man. I was curious to meet a Senator who, along with Senator Sam Brownback, were DC's "inside men" for the Religious Right, a partnership that lent credibility to the Religious Right.

Incidentally, I met Rick at his publicist's office in Leesburg, Virginia, a small, historic town within commuting distance of Capitol Hill. My cinematographer buddy Jimmy and I arrived early and walked around Leesburg, where we actually found a manger in the town square. I couldn't help but notice that this manger scene featured a blond-haired and blue-eyed Christ child.

DAN: Why is the gospel of love dividing America?

RICK You're probably best to look at Europe for an answer to that question, because you see a more advanced stage of the problem. I think what you are seeing is an increased secularization of the world. Faith is being replaced with the hard realities of science and materialism and "we don't need these ancient documents anymore."

DAN: The Age of Enlightenment sorted everything out for us—

RICK: Europe says "We're postmodern; we really have arrived as a species. We know how we got here: evolution with a god. We're little machines programmed by random chance and all we have to do is enjoy life at this point and get the most out of it for ourselves." That's where Europe is, and there is a movement in this country to follow along. And this book (the Bible) divides because it claims there is a spiritual realm, there is a Creator, and all these things America has heretofore accepted as a fact are now controversial. They (the secular movement) sound very tolerant:

"It's fine if you want to believe this stuff, just don't bring it into the public square."

DAN: My observation is that there is a group on the Far Left, the secularists let's call them; there is a group on the Far Right, perhaps you would be considered part of that group; and then there is everybody else in the middle. Those in the middle, who are the vast majority, do have ethics and values that are Judeo-Christian by definition, but they don't spend much time thinking about this stuff. Is there something about the way this perceived slide is being communicated that comes off as alarmist? Perhaps the mainstream majority would be more interested in this conversation or understand the issues better if things were presented in a different way, a less alarmist way.

RICK: There are some that sound alarmist . . . rejectionist of any reason or rational thinking so they reject the whole nature of the opposition. Whereas, the God I believe in is the God of faith, of Abraham, Isaac, and Jacob—He's also the God of reason, the God of the philosophers. A God who can and does, in fact, reveal Himself through His creation. So through science and reason and rational thinking you can arrive at some of His revelations. There are some things that take a leap of faith. When we just say, "Our God is the God of the Bible and we're right and anybody else who believes in science or materialism or anything else is just wrong or they're a threat or a danger," I disagree with that. Christianity was founded at the intersection, for the first time, of the Greeks and the Jews. Paul spread the gospel throughout the Roman Empire, so you had this synthesis of the God of the philosophers and reason and the God of Abraham and faith coming together—and Christianity is built very solidly on both. And when we get away from this "it's all divine revelation and all these other folks are wrong," then I think we're as guilty of the same crime as they (secularists) are, which is "all that matters is rational and reason and faith has no role to play." It is both. And I think that has been the key to America—we have to understand there is room for both.

DAN: The oversimplification, the "I'm right"—

RICK: Yeah, "I'm right. The Bible says this so therefore you're wrong." The classic debate we've been having over the past several years is that of evolution. The Bible does say, "here's how we were created," but God also reveals Himself through His creation and we need to examine the science and be open to that and see where that scientific discovery might take us. I think it takes more faith to believe the theory of evolution than it does to believe we were created by a divine being—but we have to look at the science. God could reveal something very different than what we are believing right now. We have to be open to the material world, we just can't be owned by it.

DAN: I recall (Nicolaus) Copernicus making a discovery or two that the church had some trouble with.

RICK: Absolutely. God gave us the minds to be able to find these things out and science is not an ethics-free zone. There is no moral neutrality in technology or science.

DAN: Looking at the core aspects of Christ's ministry you see humility, you see how He prioritizes and not only what He says but how He does it. If you were watching from a hill when Jesus went to the woman at the well, you could glean an awful lot without hearing a single word. We could pick up a couple of things from Jesus, I guess?

RICK: We sure could. Obviously, a lot of the moral questions of the day we claim ownership of those answers . . . I'm not suggesting that we don't stand up for truth, but I think we have to do so in a less condemnatory fashion.

DAN: How can we do the hot-button issues?

RICK: By asking questions. If abortion is right, for example, let's have a real discussion about the moral and worldly consequences instead of just saying, "Well, God says we can't do this" and just lay down the law. We have to engage people and help them think through the consequences. If the argument goes, "Abortion is a good thing for women because they're in a potentially tragic situation with an unwanted pregnancy, and abortion is a way to avoid a lot of pain and discomfort in their lives," then we need to understand that is a real problem. People going through this situation, it's very difficult. Christ's message was always love, and we need to approach fallen human beings, which we all are, with that constancy of love instead of judgment. If the woman at the well didn't experience the love at the first part of the story, then the "go and sin no more" at the end of the story wouldn't have had the same meaning. Jesus never backed away from the truth, but He always put it in the context of "here is someone who loves you."

One of the things I've tried to do in the course of my time in the Senate is to be someone of faith who says to conservatives and Republicans, "We have to be a movement that cares about the people Jesus cares about, who are the poor." We, the conservatives, need to show the poor we care just as much about them as everybody else in this society.

DAN: In the same vein of love instead of judgment we're talking about, what do you think the response from the gay and liberal communities would've been thirty years ago had the church responded to the AIDS crisis differently?

RICK: That's a great question. I've done a lot of work in that area; I've been the lead advocate in fundraising for the AIDS crisis, particularly overseas, and I've been criticized for doing it. "There's money that's going to be used for things we don't approve of like condoms or needle exchanges and we should stop the money from going there." I may not think that's necessarily the right long-term approach to solving the problem, but the Left were there on the front lines meeting the needs when no one else on our side was even trying. It's hard for us to come in, after they've been there for twenty years helping and say, "Oh, by the way, you're doing this wrong."

DAN: I was talking to a reporter from the *San Francisco Chronicle* who had done a story on Kaye Warren (Pastor Rick Warren's wife) and Saddleback's AIDS outreach to the gay community. He told me that the social service organizations and the gay community were a little leery: "Where have you guys been for the last twenty-five years?"

RICK: There are a lot of hard feelings out there in the gay community and those who say, "All you wanted to do was condemn us. You said 'AIDS was the scourge that was going to wipe us out because we are evil.'" And we forgot to look at these people as children of God. Yes, they made mistakes and yes, they did things that were wrong according to what we believe; but they're still children of God and that demands that we love them. We should care for them and help them instead of simply condemning them. We can condemn an action we believe is wrong, but we can never condemn the people who do it. You can condemn many of the things I've done in my life and will continue to do in all likelihood, but that doesn't mean you have the right to condemn me and not love me. You have to love me; it's what you're called to do. It's what we're all called to do, and I think we've forgotten that. It is difficult in this world because we personalize everything and when you condemn an action it's seen as condemning the person. We have to be extra-sensitive and extra-careful in this kind of world to distinguish between actions and individuals. In fact, we should go overboard because of how easily it can be twisted to appear as judgmental.

DAN: I have great empathy for your vocation because you have to reconcile, in a very public way, the gray areas of what we believe and how we act. It seems a particularly tricky business when you have to make laws on these issues, because you have to be very decisive and precise.

RICK: It is tricky. We come to the job as a representative in Congress with the responsibility, I believe, to give the person who voted for you your best judgment. When you bring your best judgment you bring everything that helps form that judgment—including all your years of education, your life experience, and your faith, which is a moral code by which you make decisions. I see far too many people, in my opinion people of faith, who feel it's appropriate to leave their faith at the door as they walk into the Senate chamber.

DAN: Whether people intellectually acknowledge it or not, faith or lack thereof informs every decision anybody makes.

RICK: How do you determine what's right or wrong without looking at some sort of moral code? Whether it's from the philosophers or whether it's from bubblegum wrappers, you get it from somewhere. And most people in America, not all, but most get it from faith. To exclude that . . . you're making decisions based on what? I always ask people, if they say their faith should have no role, then what does? Are you going to make a decision based on the "facts"? You can read anything and get twenty different interpretations. Most decisions we make have many factors involved. How do you weigh those factors? How do you do that without having some sort of hierarchy as to what's important? I don't think you can get that without having some element of faith.

DAN: Everybody bases a decision on something.

RICK: In many cases they base it on what the polls say. Their faith is based on the latest Zogby poll. That's the worst, in my opinion— to defer your judgment to a bunch of people, a sample of five hundred people, who may not know anything about the subject at hand. We see that far too often in this country, and I think it's dangerous.

DAN: Going back to "the language of America," the bite-sized slogans, I think there are a lot of people who have been turned off by "Take Back America," "Values Voters," and all "Us and Them" kinds of phrases that create unnecessary division in our country. There are people who would agree, by and large, with this so-called ultraconservative position—if the language didn't light the room on fire before the conversation started.

RICK: There's no question that tone matters. How you say it and how you look when you say it matters as much as what you say. We're a society that is a "feel" society, and when you're out there pounding the fist and pointing the finger and being self-righteous or righteous, you turn off folks in America. America wants to like the person delivering the message, and they don't want to feel threatened by them. A lot of the problems that we're having are due to the approach we're taking and not necessarily to what we're saying. If we're delivering a message that the people of America don't want to hear, then so be it. As long as we're not delivering the message in such a way that they won't listen in the first place. I think far too often we've packaged the message and the messenger in a way that turns off America before they ever get to listen.

DAN: We've been around the country asking people, "What do you think of the culture wars?" and they're like, "Huh?"

RICK: What culture wars?

DAN: Yeah.

RICK: Like you said, most Americans are comfortable and move with the flow. But the flow has become a toxic flow that erodes the kinds of things that I believe in and are traditional American values. It's the frog boiling in the water: if you throw the frog in hot water he's going to jump out, but if you just turn it up one notch at a time . . .

DAN: You know, I'm predisposed to label the culture wars as outrageous hyperbole, but that frog analogy actually makes sense. I could be that frog, it's possible.

RICK: Whether you talk about pop culture or the news media or academia, they're constantly eroding the values that I think made America great. I wrote a whole book about it called *It Takes a Family*. We have to engage in all of those spheres and try to provide an alternative view. We have to try and change the environmental quality of the water we're swimming in, because we're swimming in a very toxic pool right now.

That war is real, but it's not a war that the average person sees in that context. Even if they don't think about it daily they probably have interactions: They don't want their six-year-old seeing Viagra commercials during the game; they'd rather not have the Coors Light girls bouncing in front of their eleven-year-old boy, or have him playing violent video games. Those are the day-to-day things many parents deal with—that's their own little culture war. But they don't look at it in the big terms. They look at it in little terms, and unless we're out there on their side fight ing the little things, they're never going to join us on the big things.

DAN: You participated in Justice Sunday III.

RICK: Was that the one in Philadelphia?

DAN: Yeah.

RICK: Yes.

DAN: With a name like that I thought it was a big-time wrestling event. You didn't break a chair over anyone's head did you?

RICK: [laughs] I didn't.

DAN: One thing I know about Americans: we don't like to be told what to do or what's good for us.

RICK: We have to do it in a way that respects people instead of going out and trying to ban those things. If we do that then, "You're telling us what we can and can't watch." But if we provide you with the tools to, say, stop certain channels from coming into your house, then you have a choice. And Americans love choices. We should approach this in a way that is consistent with the American spirit: this rugged individualism where everybody can take care of themselves, which is how we like to see ourselves. And we should provide Americans with the tools to live in a more positive and wholesome world—rather than one full of sex and death and destruction and violence—by giving them alternatives that have some sizzle, but are still good. You can't just turn the bad off and not give them anything good. We need to do both.

Here's the funny thing, I would wager that most of America basically agrees with Rick Santorum's take, so the whole "Far Right whacko" label is puzzling to me. I can understand if the people of Pennsylvania didn't reelect Rick because they thought he wasn't representing their needs, but that would be the only reason that would've made sense. I hope the people of Pennsylvania didn't vote Santorum out because they thought he was a jerk or a bigot or antigay or a theocrat or any of the names thrown at him because I didn't see anything that would lead me to believe those things were true. And, even though he was a sitting U.S. Senator at the time of this interview, I was moved by his humility and his clear desire to do good things for this country.

Yeah, I know what you're thinking: *What was a guy like that doing in politics in the first place?*

Chapter Seven

michael REAGAN

The radio announced that the temperature in the Valley had eclipsed the century mark. As I stepped out of the production van onto the hot sidewalk, I estimated the temperature was closer to 200 degrees. Construction on the high-rise office building on Ventura Boulevard in Studio City, California, forced us to park half a block from the main entrance. *Great.* Killer heat, and now we were going to have to haul the gear down the street to the office where Michael Reagan broadcast his syndicated radio show.

As we were twenty minutes early, Jimmy and I thought it would be wise to find the studio, introduce ourselves, and "scout the location," as we say in the biz, to identify the bare minimum of gear we'd have to haul. This was an important decision because, as this production was a very low-budget independent film, I, the esteemed director, was also the assistant *schlepper*. Jimmy, the guy who knows what all the gear is, was of course named head schlepper.

We navigated around the yellow construction tape and found a way into the building. A few moments later we poked our heads into a nondescript-looking suite of offices. Searching for some kind of clue, I noticed the words "The Michael Reagan Show" emblazoned across a blue wall behind the desk. I took a leap and assumed the genial looking man at the desk was, in fact, Michael Reagan.

"Mike?"

"Yeah?"

Why is he looking at me like I'm crazy? We're only ten minutes early, well within interview etiquette.

"Hi, I'm Dan and this is Jimmy. We're here from the documentary film," I said even as I searched his eyes, trying to understand his confused look.

"Oh, is that today?"

I smiled. "I hope so."

"I can't today. I'm doing *Hannity and Colmes* tonight; I have another interview to do in a half-hour." He shrugged.

"Well, we came from Oregon to talk to you. Would it be possible to talk in the half-hour before your call-in interview?" I asked not quite begging, but inching ever closer.

Reagan smiled, apparently scoring points by not flinching at the obvious change of plans. "Okay, you can have a half-hour," he said.

Relieved, I still asked for a little clarification, "When does that half-hour start?"

"You're burning the interview time right now."

"Okay"—I laughed—"we'll hurry."

I looked at Jimmy and shrugged—then we bolted for the door. We sprinted down the office corridors, careful not to upend the lawyers and accountants who foolishly had chosen this time to stroll to the lobby for an afternoon beverage.

We scooped up the gear, overloading ourselves so as to get everything on one trip. Jimmy and I were soaked with sweat as we waddled through the construction zone and down the hall to the elevators. We were both laughing, because what else are you going to do? We finally got into the elevators and they seemed to take forever to reach the fifth floor (okay, I don't remember which floor it was but grant me a little artistic license, will ya). I was reminded of that moment from *The Blues Brothers* where Jake and Elwood, with all of the Illinois law enforcement community in hot pursuit, stand in the elevator of the Federal Building and take the longest elevator ride ever. A Muzak version of "The Girl from Ipanema" began to play in my head. (I swear it did.)

Jimmy set a low-budget production land-speed record in setting up the gear. I helped him as much as I could without getting in the way and searched the surroundings for any clues as to how the interview might go. I spied a framed photo of Michael with Ann Coulter. I saw a huge picture of the aircraft carrier USS *Ronald Reagan* named, of course, for the fortieth president of the United States and the man (along with actress Jane Wyman) who adopted Michael. I noticed a stack of Michael Reagan's new book *Twice Adopted,* and a poster of his 1997 book *A City on a Hill.*

"We're good," Jimmy gasped.

Michael positioned himself under the boom microphone and affected an upper-crust accent, Elizabeth era if I had to guess: "Oh, mother, mother, can you hear me?" Playing with microphones is always fun. That's probably why he was doing radio—fun with the mike. I laughed and realized our hustle and good-natured approach had endeared us to Michael.

"If I'd remembered this was today, I would've worn a different shirt. Is this okay?"

"It's fine," I answered a little too quickly. The mood was light, but I suspected we had only ten minutes until his phone interview would be calling in.

DAN:	Our film is called *Lord, Save Us From Your Followers*—
MICHAEL:	[laughs] Save me from me.
DAN:	Exactly. Self-awareness isn't something we do very well. I want to know why the gospel of love is dividing America. What's going on?
MICHAEL:	Many of us believe if you had Christian values put back into America that somehow all of this [conflict] would, in fact, change. We have more fatherless homes that we've ever had in the history of man. But if you look at the culture, the culture uplifts that. When a Hollywood star breaks up with her husband or his wife it's uplifted like it's the greatest thing on the planet. They [media] don't look at it like, "You just broke up a marriage." So you have young girls all over the planet who

think *Well, it's okay, you don't have to get married or divorce isn't a big deal.* And parents are in this battle to say, "No, there are values in America, there are morals in America." We need to get back to those morals.

DAN: When we were talking before, you mentioned three numbers: twenty-four, forty-three, and fourteen.

MICHAEL: Good memory.

DAN: What is the significance of those numbers?

MICHAEL: I talk a lot to pro-life groups, crisis pregnancy groups (being adopted myself) and twenty-four represents the percentage of young girls who get abortions who say they're Catholic, forty-three represents the percentage of young girls who get abortions who say they're Protestant, and fourteen represents the percentage of young girls who get abortions who say they're evangelical/born-again Christians. So my question to these groups is, "Why are you looking to the government to pass a law to stop your daughters from getting abortions?" What are we doing wrong in our own households that is causing our daughters to go out and get these abortions? We have to look inward, and so often we look outward. "We are holier than thou, we don't make mistakes, we're Godly, we go to church on Sunday," so we've done nothing wrong; yet our daughters are more fearful of telling us they are pregnant than they are of the abortionists.

DAN: You add those numbers up and that's 71 percent. With all this us versus them talk going around, are we the "us" *and* the "them"?

MICHAEL: We are the us and the them and we don't want to see it. We can all quote John 3:16, we think it's great God sent His Son to die for our sins. But what father, what mother is willing to put themselves on the cross for their children? I talk to people all the time on my radio show, "If my daughter gets pregnant, I'm kicking her out of the house." Well you just sent her to the abortionist. Or "I'm an elder, I'm a deacon in the church, you are an embarrassment to me." We have to start looking inward and see what we can do to change the dynamics.

DAN: A little humility goes a long way.

MICHAEL: Absolutely.

DAN: With many of these hot-button issues it seems like we're having the wrong conversation. Is intelligent design the proper rebuttal to evolution? Is a pro-life argument the proper rebuttal to the stem cell question?

MICHAEL: We allowed ourselves to get pulled into a pro-life/pro-choice argument. We get pulled into these things and we forget to look at the facts, the actual background of the issues. What's happened is "you're Christian, you're Republican, you're against stem cell research." That's furthest from the truth.

DAN: So you're for stem cell research?

MICHAEL: Nobody on the planet is against stem cell research, and there's no law against stem cell research, whether adult or embryonic, only the federal government has put the brakes on. But there are questions about embryonic stem cell research; lab rats and lab mice are getting tumors. There's no law against embryonic stem cell research or any kind of stem cell research, but the government puts speed limits on everything they get involved with. The private sector has been giving hundreds of millions of dollars to stem cell research, but the embryonic side is drying up because these companies see the bad science and they see lawsuits. The majority of the money is going into adult stem cell research, which by the way, is helping with about seventy-two different diseases around the world today, but you never hear about that. And if you say anything against them, then somehow you're against God, country, mom, and apple pie.

DAN: My psychic powers tell me there are a lot of agenda-driven positions in these issues.

MICHAEL: It's a great way to raise money. [laughs]

DAN: I received a letter from a conservative Christian activist group that informed me that no longer was gay marriage the primary threat to Western civilization, but it was now the Muslims.

MICHAEL: I think it's the gay Muslims.

DAN: [laughs] Yes, and I think we should lock arms together and march against the gay Muslims right now. We could save Western civilization. But here's the question: Does Jesus even care about saving Western civilization? It wasn't even here when Jesus was on earth.

MICHAEL: I think Jesus cares about everybody individually. And we have to be a light to the world. And there are battles that you fight. I understand that, but we have to take care of our own house. Today I can't find a church that doesn't have an outreach program, and I can't find one that doesn't need an in-reach program. Everybody wants to become a megachurch—I'm bigger than you, I'm better than you. But I sit there in prayer circles in church and there are a lot of hurting people in churches today. We gotta heal the people in the churches and through that we can heal the world.

DAN: We can do both outreach and in-reach simultaneously, can't we?

MICHAEL: You've got to heal your own first. You can't send me out sick and expect me to heal the sick, "I'm sick! Heal me."

DAN: Okay, interesting. I wanted to ask you about how the definition of *Christian* has changed from the Christian president in 1980, your father, and the current President George W. Bush. How has religion and politics changed in those years?

MICHAEL: The Christian community finally said, "We've had it." We've really had it with secularism, and if we don't get mad and stand up and start saying something, it's not going to get better—it's going to get worse. We have to fight for those things we believe in, that's why the fight against gay marriage. The gay community feels like they have a civil right to marriage and to deny that right goes against the Constitution. But if you open it up to them, you have to open it up to everybody.

Right about here in the interview, I became aware of a loud beeping noise. I looked around assuming it was something in Reagan's office. But he was looking at me as if I should know what the sound was. *Uh-oh, it's a camera battery alarm.*

"That was a fresh battery," Jimmy said. I heard him mutter a curse word under his breath to commemorate the surprising death of a freshly-charged battery. (I should mention when Jimmy cusses with his Kansas accent it neutralizes any offensiveness inherent in the word. I think it's the same linguistic property at work when Hugh Grant drops a curse word with his charming British accent and not a soul is offended.)

Jimmy scrambled down to the production van for a new battery while I chatted with Reagan and prayed for Jimmy to return before the time-challenged Reagan's scheduled phone interview. After a few moments, Michael's producer appeared in the doorway, "Sorry it's time."

I sat motionless. We maybe had enough footage for a few good sound bites, but this guy was really spirited and, selfishly, I was having fun talking to him. Reagan didn't answer immediately; I averted my eyes and held my breath.

Finally, Reagan said, "Tell them to call back in five or ten minutes. We're not quite finished." The producer offered no protest, and I had my reprieve.

A moment later Jimmy came huffing and puffing in and slapped the battery onto the camera. Yes, I confess, I had sent the smoker down the block to the production van. I believe I was justified in this decision because I was in better shape and Jimmy needed the exercise. No, I'm kidding. Sure, I would beat Jimmy in a race to the van, but I'd spend a half-hour trying to figure out which thing was the battery.

The camera hummed and a picture flickered to life on the monitor.

Reagan looked up, "We good?"

"You know what? Thanks." Jimmy said as he extended his hand to Michael.

"No problem," Reagan laughed.

"You could've made me look really bad today, but you didn't and I appreciate it."

Jimmy was still wheezing heavily, but we were going to lose Reagan soon, so I proceeded. But if you're a person who loves those "behind-the-scenes" stories, months later, when I was reviewing the footage I became aware of this heavy breathing during the interview. I literally stopped the clip and looked around the room—where was that breathing coming from? I hit play and the breathing, which sounded like a prank caller, resumed and then it hit me: it was the completely winded Jimmy, leaning over the camera to operated gasping into the on-board camera microphone. I flipped off the audio on channel one and Jimmy's iron lung ceased.

Jimmy's hustle bought us the final ten minutes of the interview.

DAN: Let's talk for a minute about money and power. What happens if we get prayer back into school? We won't have anything to fight about.

MICHAEL: You're absolutely right. I get calls on my show and I say, "Okay, fine, prayer is no longer allowed in school. When was the last time you prayed with your child before they went off to school?" And, the other side of the coin is, there's money in fighting all these issues. And I wonder sometimes if they want the issue to go away because if it does, where will the money come from?

DAN: In First John it talks about how Jesus came in "truth and grace." Seems like we might be a little heavy on the "truth" and a little light with the "grace."

MICHAEL: Sometimes we don't look at ourselves, and we do look hypocritical. We absolutely do. Last time I went to church they weren't talking about pornography from the pulpit. They don't talk about adultery from the pulpit or spousal abuse, none of these things—and there are a lot of people sitting there who are living through this stuff who are in pain. It's hard to give grace when your congregation is not dealing with the issues they're in pain over. Christ could give that grace because He understood our pain, but we get self-absorbed sometimes.

DAN: Is that why the gay marriage issue became such a hot button? Because there aren't that many gay people, the issue doesn't directly relate to too many people.

MICHAEL: You could make an argument that most gays don't want to get married. There's the activist group that is the counterpart to the Religious Right. You know, the Dobsons, Falwells, Robertsons have their counterpart on the left and they're making the loudest noise. Television shows us gay pride parades, Dykes on Bikes, and we're all appalled by it—so are most gays. They're embarrassed by it. But they're afraid to go on TV and say anything for fear of being ostracized by their own community. There are all kinds of dynamics going on here, but the fact is most gays don't want to get married. We need to quit listening to the factions within the gay community that are driving the bus.

DAN: What about the handful who do want to get married?

MICHAEL: If you open marriage up to the gays, then you have to open it up to everyone. There has to be a pillars and I think God put it there biblically. We have to look at this biblically because every society, historically, that has gone down that other road has been destroyed, absolutely destroyed. In New York the other day, they announced that transgenders can now use whatever bathroom they want. *Hello?*

DAN: I missed that one.

MICHAEL: That's a little bit outrageous. I can go to work on Friday as Michael and Monday as Michelle, but you can't discriminate against me as long as I'm dressed gender appropriate? Give me a break. Some of these things are laughable, but, of course, you can't laugh or you get sued. But you gotta take stands. If you don't stand for something you'll fall for anything.

DAN: But you can't legislate against crazy, can you? If a man wants to marry his dog isn't he just insane? What are you going to do?

MICHAEL: You're right. When you say that it reminds me of when my dad got shot. I asked the Secret Service agent, "How do you let that happen?" He says, "Mike, we train twenty-four hours a day to be ready to protect the president of the United States against people shooting him, but you can never train long enough or hard enough to protect him against the crazies." There are crazies in this world, but we can't allow the crazies to run it.

Choosing not to push Reagan's hospitality to the limit, I wrapped up the interview before the producer returned. But as we were wrapping our gear, our new, good friend Michael regaled us with stories and, frankly, made us feel right at home. He invited us to hang out while he jumped on the phone for a ten-minute interview for someone else's radio show, and then the visit continued. Before sending us back into the Southern California heat, Michael gave us each an autographed copy of *Twice Adopted,* a fitting parting gift to our speed interview.

Directing this film has brought myriad blessings to me, and one of them is meeting people like Michael who have had a fascinating life and are willing to share their experiences with me (and you).

Chapter Eight

sister mary timothy
AND THE CHRISTIANS

As he walked down the sidewalk toward me, I first noticed the cigarette dangling precariously in his left hand. No wait, it was the robe, my eye was first drawn to the flowing black robe. Since he was the only person strolling through San Francisco's Castro District on a sunny spring day wearing a robe, he was bound to stand out—though no one else on the street seemed to take notice. With each stride the robe would swish left then right, just barely grazing along the sidewalk, gently brushing across stray blades of grass that had managed to push up through the cracks.

I actually began to grow a little self-conscious, because next to him my jeans and blue-and-white striped button-down shirt (that my wife had bought at the Gap) were downright pedestrian. Actually, let me start this again. As I think about it, my eye was first pulled in by the shocking white, kabuki-base makeup accented artfully by green eye shadow and little plastic glitter gems that adorned his cheeks. As he grew closer, the skill and care of this makeup job became increasingly apparent. He smiled at me and none of the jewels fell off his face. Wow. No wonder he was ten minutes late; the guys from KISS require a team of makeup artists and hair stylists to create this same sort of dramatic, eye-popping effect. Of course, no hair stylist was required on this job as a nun's habit with an orchid in the center neatly framed his face . . . you know, I may have noticed the nun's habit first. At any rate, I can tell you I had never seen a grown man dressed as a nun and made up like a clown. As he extended his hand I noted that he was probably six foot one or maybe two; I hadn't expected that he would be taller than me. Strangely, this physical characteristic was as unsettling as the others, which is saying something because I grew up with an aversion to clowns and always found nuns to be cold and intimidating.

Sister Mary Timothy's friendly, unpretentious voice didn't fit with the rest of the dramatic presentation. "I'm so sorry to keep you waiting."

"No problem." I smiled. His voice was deeper than it had sounded on the phone, but its gentle resonance and lyrical flow seemed to soften the masculine features. Sister Mary Timothy fumbled with a key, unlocked the gate, and led me into a beautiful urban garden.

"It takes about two hours to manifest, but it took me longer today because my dog kept jumping up on my lap." He laughed. I nodded. *A dog person, eh? Figures. Clowns, nuns, and dog people—now I had three prejudices to set aside while I interviewed this character who could have rolled right out of a Roald Dahl nightmare.* (You'll remember Dahl invented the Oompa Loompa's from *Charley and the Chocolate Factory.*) Sister Mary Timothy could've jumped center for Willy Wonka's basketball team.

"Manifest?"

"Oh, I don't walk around like this all the time," he laughed.

We moved through the garden, maneuvering around the raised flowerbeds.

"That one's mine." The robe fluttered as he gestured. "I spread my friend's ashes in that one," he said matter-of-factly, though I heard a sad resignation in a simple sentence.

As we took our seats opposite each other on a raised wooden deck, I noticed how much more warm and accessible Sister Mary Timothy seemed when compared to the first time I'd seen his screaming face in an Associated Press photo on the Internet. My live and in-person observation was informed by his nervousness to be seated before an interviewer and his film crew and also by his willingness to share with me what had driven him to explode at a group of Christian teenagers singing hymns, praying quietly, and otherwise minding their own business . . . at a rally on the steps of city hall in San Francisco, California, entitled Battle Cry: Fight for a Generation.

The inaugural Battle Cry stadium event drew twenty-five thousand teens from all over Northern California to the City by the Bay for a weekend of concerts, sermons, and a little rally that erupted into a loud, hyperbole festival.

DAN: What was your understanding of what Battle Cry had come to do? Why had someone alerted you?

SISTER MARY
TIMOTHY: Because it was Christians coming to the city, which felt like condemning us, and when we got there that's what it felt like. We didn't go there to scream and yell, at least I didn't. I went there to stand my ground. This is my city, this is a place that I call home, and they were shipping thousands upon thousands of children, not adults, to fight the battle. They didn't have any antigay stuff on their Web site; they were anti-materialism, but the thing that struck me really funny was, I saw on the news that night, on their opening night of song and praise, Ron Luce came on stage in a Hummer. That's a little contradictory. You're against materialism and sensationalism and you're coming in on a Hummer with fireworks shooting. Come on. If you want to speak the word of Christ, then speak the word of Christ.

To better understand the reason behind these events I traveled to the Lindale, Texas, campus of Teen Mania Ministries to meet Battle Cry founder Ron Luce and hear more about his mission to lead a movement of teens to fight for their generation against the distorting influence of the media and the culture.

RON LUCE: We have parents, community, church that have surrounded us to help us raise our kids—but now so much of the technology and media bypasses so much of that natural protection and whether it's the Internet or the iPod or advertisers, it gets right to the kid. Some are saying, "This is the first generation to be shaped more outside the home than inside the home." The first generation in the history of the world.

DAN: So what really happened? There are a few hundred Battle Cry kids, about fifty protestors and you're divided by a ten-foot barrier or something, right? And they're just singing songs or praying?

SISTER MARY
TIMOTHY: Their sound system wasn't too good, so I couldn't really hear their speeches too clearly, but I was talking to this one guy who kept saying, "We love you, we love you—and we're praying for you."

And I said, "That's really nice, but I don't need you to pray for me. My life is perfectly blessed. I have a roof over my head, I have clothes on my back, I have food in my stomach, and I have people around who love me. But you should probably pray for those who need prayers. No offense, I appreciate you wanting to pray for me."

And he says, "But I love you, and I want you to come away from this lifestyle."

And I said, "It's not a lifestyle, buddy, it's my life." I was standing with my husband, and I said, "This is the man I married two years ago on these city hall steps, and here's your group coming here to my city preaching what you preach against us. You know, that homosexuality is wrong, Leviticus whatever, Sodom and Gomorrah, blah blah blah, I've heard it three million times before. I'm tired of it, come up with something new." I probably wouldn't have gone—or made a big deal of it—if they weren't on the city hall steps.

DAN: Let's talk about how you got from "thanks for praying for me" to the picture I saw. What was said to you?

SISTER MARY
TIMOTHY: It wasn't so much anything that was said to me. I was yelling at
              this one older woman in the middle of the crowd who looked
              at me and kept mouthing, "I'm going to pray for you, I'm going
              to pray for you, I'm going to pray for you." And I'm like, "I can't
              take it anymore," and I fell into human nature. When you feel
              provoked or threatened you stand up for yourself. It's not your
              life, it's mine. I'm not going to your backyard and saying, "You
              shouldn't grow those tomatoes" or whatever. But if you look at
              that picture I look like an angry man or angry nun, drag
              queen—I am a nun, not a drag queen—but from the outside
              that's what it would look like, this angry man with these things
              on his head who's screaming at a bunch of kids.

                  I left that protest, and I had a migraine for two days
              from screaming so much. I felt horrible that I was yelling at all
              these children.

For his side, Luce was caught off guard by the protest, though San
Francisco's strident liberal public posturing, from the flower power of
Haight-Ashbury to the Dykes on Bikes of the gay pride parades, would seem
to be pretty well established.

RON LUCE: I actually heard the people before I saw them. I heard them
              shouting, and I thought, "What's going on?" It's like we put our
              finger in a beehive, and we didn't know it. We didn't realize it
              was kind of a hotbed for a very violent response to people who
              represent the Bible. A reporter asked me, "What do you think
              about these homosexuals?" And most of them were men
              dressed as women, and I said, "Oh, we love homosexuals. Now
              we don't like what they do, we don't like their lifestyle, but we
              love them as people." This was such a stark contrast, they were
              calling us angry, yet they were the ones who were angry.

     DAN: Since the Battle Cry protest was pretty gentle, what do you
              think the protestors were reacting to?

RON LUCE: They probably had somebody who called themselves a

Christian really mistreat them, and now they think that's what all Christians are like.

While at Luce's headquarters in Texas we had the chance to visit with a few of the college-age kids who were attending the Teen Mania Ministries Honor Academy. One young woman, Naomi, was actually a camera operator at the Battle Cry rally.

DAN: The reaction of the protestors was pretty strong. What did that tell you?

NAOMI: It tells me that the Christians they run in to are hypocritical: they say they love God, and they do everything for God, but they don't love His people.

I don't know if I agree with Ron Luce's diagnosis of society's ills and I'm not sure about his remedy, but I sure liked what Naomi and some of her classmates had to say, so there may be something good happening out there in Texas. Yeah, I'm trying to be balanced here—sure I hold the Christians to a high bar, but we claim to follow Jesus and that's a pretty high standard—but there was another detail in this conflict too ironic to ignore.

DAN: I did find it amazing that a city commissioner got involved making some kind of official proclamation that Battle Cry wasn't welcome in San Francisco.

SISTER MARY
TIMOTHY: It was Mark Leno, I believe, and he's come under attack a little bit for that. I saw him two days later at an event and said, "You know we support you, Mark."

DAN: But if San Francisco is a tolerant city, and it seems to be, shouldn't the tolerance go both ways? Isn't tolerance, tolerance?

SISTER MARY
TIMOTHY: They have every right to come here and preach what they think is right, and I'm not saying that I'm right—the only

time I think I'll find out what's right and wrong is the day I die. Until then I can only live up to what's true in my heart, and I know this is our home. You have all of middle America; you have all of the South. And it's not like "you need to stay over there and we'll stay over here." We have to be able to come to a point where we either learn to play nice or let be.

At least these young people are taking a stand for something. I have to at least give them that.

Us against them can't be the only choices, right? That's part of why we did this movie, why I wrote this book; there's just so much us versus them, all the time, it's wearing me out.

RON LUCE: We live in a "Christian nation," but we have a very un-Christian culture; we have a culture that's violently opposed to Christian values. And part of that is because people who have faith and values haven't spoken up very much so people without faith and without biblical values have spoken up, and whoever speaks up, they get to shape the culture. They win.

And though Battle Cry made no specific antigay comment, the symbolism of their city hall rally seemed obvious to everyone else. Though, in fairness, the city hall steps are used by everyone from PETA to the American Cancer Society to the Girl Scouts, so why not the Christians? Yes, it's all fair, but is this about fair or about connecting with those who need to hear the Good News? So, even without intended malice, choosing city hall for the Battle Cry rally did nothing to quell discord. And for the record, I asked Ron why Battle Cry didn't choose a more relevant mass media target.

RON LUCE: It wasn't "in your face" about how city hall had been used in the past; it was more like we have an event here and give us time we'll get to Hollywood and Madison Avenue. It needs to be pointed out that these forces are shaping, in a very destructive way, our young people.

As it turns out, Battle Cry returned a second time to San Francisco in March 2007 and again held a rally on the city hall steps. Clearly, Battle Cry's agenda for this event had little to do with reconciliation, and perhaps the spectacle of confrontation is good for morale or fund-raising or something.

I was disappointed to hear Ron Luce on James Dobson's *Focus on the Family* radio broadcast the next week and hear the story told in self-serving terms. Dobson at one point said something to the effect of "You held a rally on the city hall steps and were confronted by the very face of evil." I deeply resented that sweeping caricature—especially because in the middle of my interview with Sister Mary Timothy I was struck by a basic yet profound understanding: God *loves* Sister Mary Timothy as much as He loves me. Think about that a minute. This guy, in this crazy getup, is loved by the Creator as much as I am. We gotta get this one right people; we have to understand this context or we're going to be running in circles forever.

While Battle Cry showed up and did the same drill in '07, the Sisters of Perpetual Indulgence and other Left-leaning protestors chose not to repeat their screams of protest. Sister Mary Timothy sent this note following Battle Cry's return.

> . . . this year instead of protesting Battle Cry, we held a Joyfest instead. We found that our interactions with them from the year before left us feeling horrible about our actions . . . mostly us yelling at a bunch of children caught in a cross fire called religion . . . we gathered all together and when we approached the crowd, we handed out flowers and welcomed each of them to our city. We also handed out book marks that read literal translations of the Bible and what they

would mean in today's time. We left there that day and ended with a ritual back in the Castro. . . .

Can't wait to see the movie. . . .

Blessings,
Sister Mary Timothy

When we get into these ethical/moral debates it is very easy to demonize people or even, more simply, forget they are people. Because I was having a hard time getting my mind around Tim's "manifestation" as Sister Mary Timothy, it was important to me to try and understand him as a person. I really did want to get to know him a little and, generously, he shared with me that his mother died when he was four and his dad and stepmother struggled with drug addiction.

SISTER MARY
TIMOTHY: I came out at a young age. I was one of those types who couldn't really hide it. I didn't want to hide it. My father used to say he had four daughters. But my dad has taken a huge one-eighty because two years ago when I got married, I asked him to give me away—this is the man who didn't speak to me for three months after I came out when I was fifteen. When I came down to the bottom of the stairs he said to me, "Timmy, you look so beautiful. Treat each other well, love each other all the time." When he left the wedding that night he told me, "You are by far the richest man I know." For my father to say that—I was the little art freak, gay boy; I wanted to be a ballet dancer; I had HIV by the time I was seventeen—all these things and I'm the one who is the richest. My father thinks I'm the richest, that is a gift.

DAN: How did that make you feel when he said that to you?

SISTER MARY
TIMOTHY: I cried. I looked at my husband and he started to cry. I started crying. It was amazing.

DAN: You're married. What do you think are the key components to a happy marriage?

SISTER MARY
TIMOTHY: Friendship. Friendship is one of the most important qualities I share with my husband. And honesty, no matter how much it hurts, you need to be honest.

DAN: How does your marriage affect my marriage?

SISTER MARY
TIMOTHY: It doesn't. I don't think the sky is going to fall down or lightning is going to strike or crops are going to die or there's going to be famine because I'm in love with my husband and we say we're married. Marriage is much more than the legal thing. If I never get back the official document, I'm still going to be married because my soul says I'm married. My heart says, "I'm married."

DAN: Today, I'm trying not to make Jesus look bad, not to set the bar too low. How do you think things would've been different, if the church had sponsored the first few AIDS hospices in the early eighties?

SISTER MARY
TIMOTHY: They would've been showing Christ's love, honestly and truly. It shouldn't have mattered that people were gay; it shouldn't have mattered that people were suffering disfiguring diseases. They would've set their fear aside, they would've opened their hearts and done the work that needed to be done.

Sister Mary Timothy and I spoke for nearly two hours. It was hard to hear how we had let Timothy and his community down. I didn't like hearing that we believers had succumbed to fear, but we had failed our brothers and sisters. But I can't tell you how valuable being open to the conversation was for me . . . yeah, the wacky getup took a little getting used to, but I absolutely left the garden that day feeling like I'd made a new friend.

SISTER MARY
TIMOTHY: I come from an Irish Catholic and Southern Baptist background, and my grandmother on my father's side was the last

one I came out to in the family when I was fifteen. She's the Southern Baptist. She would always pray with us before she got off the phone with us or we left her presence. You know, "God please be with Timmy . . ."—I want to tell you how I came out to her because this kinda ties into the Battle Cry stuff. I wish I'd made this sign . . . my grandmother had this sign on her refrigerator since I was knee-high to a grasshopper that said, "God Don't Make No Junk," and there's this picture of a little boy pouting. God don't make no junk.

When I came out to her she asked me, "Why was I the last one to know, Timmy?"

And I said, "Well, Grams, I was a little afraid, you know your people—'Burn the gays,' 'You're going to hell' kind of stuff."

So I was really scared to tell her. But she marched me into the kitchen and made me read that sign. Then she had me come back into the living room and sit down next to her.

"Now what did the sign say?"

And I said, "God don't make no junk."

And she goes, "So, as far as you know, did God make you?"

I said, "As far as I know, probably, yeah."

"And what is my job as your grandmother on this earth?"

"To love me?"

And she says, "Where does it say I need to hate you or condemn you to hell?" She said, "Christ didn't teach any of that stuff. If God has a problem with you being gay, you'll find out at the pearly gates when you die. It's not for me to pass judgment on you. It's only my job to love you and care for you."

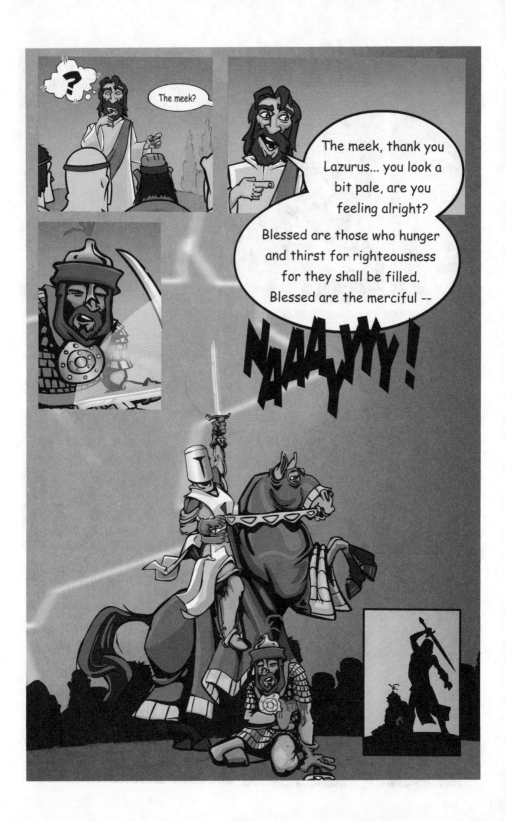

Chapter Ten

the continuing adventures of BUMPER-STICKER MAN

Our communication model is broken. In this consumer culture we've been trained to accept ad slogans, labels, sound bites, and bumper-sticker slogans as adequate. These micro-blips of information reduce the complexity of an issue, strip essential meaning from it, and ultimately snuff out conversation. "Coke—It's the Real Thing" doesn't invite you into a dialogue about the pros and cons of Coke or a discussion on the attributes of Royal Crown Cola—it just says, "Buy a Coke." "It's Adam and Eve not Adam and Steve" doesn't address the financial or social issues attendant to the same-sex marriage issue or invite a dialogue on a complex issue, it just says, "Shut up already."

This simplistic, one-way communication style we've developed seems to give us permission to be close-minded and dismissive. It does matter how you tell the story.

To create a group called Value Voters infers that everybody else is without values.

The Reverend Jerry Falwell once explained that the name Moral Majority didn't mean to infer that everyone else was the Immoral Minority, but that's what it sounded like, and, that is how people took

121

it. So if the result of the communication yields an incorrect or inaccurate perception, we should consider a new way to explain the story.

Now, of course, both *us* and *them* are guilty of this reductionism. But if we're trying to live like Jesus—represent Him—then we have to elevate our game. You can scream: "Theocracy!" or "The Religious Right is subverting the Constitution!" or "I will fight the Hollywood agenda!" or "We must win this battle to reclaim America!" and the nature of this strident, confrontational language makes us all feel we're in the right and our enemy will be defeated. And there it is: this one-way communication creates enemies rather than dealing with the issues or, more importantly, demonstrating Christ's love.

This is the United States of America and our Founding Fathers were smart guys. They knew that with the kind of freedom America was to have there would be disagreements. So Adams, Franklin, Jefferson, and the rest put safeguards in place. They created a venue in which two opposing sides could work out their points of view in full view of the population . . . that's right, I'm talking about the bumper sticker. Okay, my history might be a little off, but this fundamentalist versus secular struggle has been going on for a while. Bill Maher—comedian, host of HBO's *Real Time with Bill Maher,* and noted anti-Christian liberal monster—once commented that he was only the latest in a long line of people who believe organized religion is a mass-psychosis.

Bill's right, not necessarily about the psychosis part, but he *is* just the latest. This modern era of Christian mistrust of media and public discourse dates back to the summer of 1925 and the famous tongue lashing that columnist H. L. Mencken gave to fundamentalist Christians as he covered the Scopes Monkey Trial.

Mencken wrote for the *Baltimore Evening Sun,* July 27, 1925:

> The way to deal with superstition is not to be polite to it, but to tackle it with all arms, and so rout it, cripple it, and make it forever infamous and ridiculous. Is it, perchance, cherished by persons who should know better? Then their folly should be brought out into the light of day, and exhibited there in all its hideousness until they flee from it, hiding their heads in shame.

Oh yeah, H. L., if you're so smart, why don't you have a real first name? Huh?

Mencken churned out article after article and not all of it is as charitable. This gives you some idea of the genesis of "Liberal Media Elite." No wonder believers chose to keep faith a more private matter. But in recent years, as expressions of faith in political life were warmly received by many, Christians in America began to step back into the public discourse . . . albeit with baby steps.

The ichthys or Jesus Fish, a first-century Christian symbol, reimaged as a metallic car emblem, began to appear on automobiles across the U.S. in the '90s. What was initiated as a declaration of faith was quickly and cleverly countered by the Bill Maher fan club.

The Jesus Fish evolved, in fine Mencken tradition, by sprouting legs and crawling from the primordial ooze and onto car bumpers everywhere, marking an escalation in hostilities.

Not to be outdone, the Christians followed the "survival of the fittest" motif and returned fire with the Truth Fish, which made lunch out of Darwin. *Hah.* Take that, secular humanists!

Oh, er, wait, hang on. Here comes T. Rex, to eat the Truth Fish. This, I gotta say, doesn't really work because the T. Rex became extinct and scientists have now decided that the Tyrannosaurus rex only ate veggies. But an industry sprang to life and the debate continued.

So where has all this gotten us? The Christians are annoyed because they feel their beliefs are being mocked . . . which, of course, they are. It's interesting that this fish, this decorative statement of faith, translates to many as an attack, as "nah, nah, I'm going to heaven and you're going to hell." Intended or not, a climate of us versus them was being fostered by the very people charged with spreading the Good News to the world. Our message is often misunderstood, and I think we can do better. The question now becomes, "Does the burden fall on my lips or their ears?"

The *Lord, Save Us* . . . road show rolled into Dallas, Texas, the heart of the Bible Belt. Just south of Dallas is an idyllic American small town called Waxahachie. The gorgeous Main Street, adjacent the historic town square, seemed like an appropriate counterpoint to New York City's Times Square. So I donned the Bumper-Sticker Man suit and went in search of more answers.

The first person I met, Linda, was in her late fifties and I noticed her watching from a nearby shop window as I flubbed my lines to a stand-up over and over. Jimmy started to go hoarse shouting, "Back to one!" Fortunately, Linda came out to investigate and we played Five Questions.

DAN: How did the universe begin?
LINDA: God created the universe.
DAN: Where will you go when you die?
LINDA: Heaven.
DAN: Name something Jesus is known for.
LINDA: Creating the world.
DAN: Name something Christians are known for.
LINDA: Loving Jesus.
DAN: What's going on with the culture wars? Where's the trouble coming from?
LINDA: Non-believers.

Staking out the town square at lunchtime, I met Kyle—he of the ten-gallon cowboy hat and a belt buckle like the grill on a Cadillac Coupe de Ville—and hit him with the questions.

DAN: How did the universe begin?
KYLE: God created the universe.

DAN: Where will you go when you die?

KYLE: Heaven.

DAN: Why?

KYLE: 'Cause I'm a born-again Christian.

DAN: Name something Jesus is known for.

KYLE: Giving His life up for our sins.

DAN: Name something Christians are known for.

KYLE: Trying to live the right life, do the right thing.

DAN: What is the biggest battle of the culture wars?

KYLE: That's a tough one there. I don't know. I just think we need to get God back in America and everything's gonna be all fine.

DAN: Actually one more question: Was replacing Drew Bledsoe a mistake or is Tony Romo going to do the job?

KYLE: Romo's going to get the Cowboys back to the Super Bowl.

DAN: Enough of this religion talk, let's talk football. Cool, Kyle, thanks so much.

KYLE: You bet, brother.

I met Tim—thirties, burly, a sweet-faced fella with a quick smile—when he and his crew were setting up a holiday display on the lawn of the Waxahachie town square. The politically correct display was absent baby Jesus and mostly populated with characters from a Dickensian holiday fantasy.

DAN: We've been talking to folks about all the arguing about religion and politics. Have you been hearing some of what's been going on?

TIM: Not really, we've been trying to stay away from that. That's why our display is about the holidays and not religion.

DAN: How did the universe begin?

TIM: I guess with Adam and Eve, I would say. Others say star combustions, but I'll go with Adam and Eve.

DAN: Where will you go when you die?

TIM: Hopefully, I'll go to heaven. I think I'll go. I'm kind to people and I'm generous. I can't give away everything I have, but I'm pretty generous.

DAN: Name something Jesus is known for.

TIM: Dying for my sins.

DAN: Name something Christians are known for.

TIM: Teachers of His Word and the way He lived.

DAN: If Jesus came back today would He vote Republican or Democrat?

TIM: Democrat for sure.

DAN: Why?

TIM: Because He saved me, and that's what I think being a Democrat is all about: helping the people. So I think He'd be a Democrat.

To complete our balanced, demographic survey, here is how Lorinda—early thirties, big pretty eyes, and a warm smile—answered our five questions.

DAN: How did the universe begin?

LORINDA: God created the universe.

DAN: Where will you go when you die?

LORINDA: Heaven. [laughs]

DAN: I said "five questions," not five "hard questions."

LORINDA: Yeah, these are easy. Okay, three.

DAN: Name something Jesus is known for.

LORINDA: Walking on water.

DAN: Name something Christians are known for.

LORINDA: Compassion.

DAN: If Jesus came back today would He vote Republican or Democrat?

LORINDA: He wouldn't care. He'd be hanging out with all the discarded.

Cody was not the kind of cat I expected to meet in Waxahachie. In his midtwenties with long blond hair, loose beard, and kind eyes, he was so laid back I almost fell asleep talking with him.

DAN: How did the universe begin?

CODY: Evolution. I believe in that theory. Little stuff here and there all combined to make us.

DAN: Where will you go when you die?

CODY: I do believe in reincarnation. You choose what you want to come back as or you just float forever in peace.

DAN: Name something Jesus is known for.

CODY: He died for all of us, up on that cross getting brutalized . . . it was just wrong.

DAN: Name something Christians are known for.

CODY: Unyielding faith.

DAN: If Jesus came back today would He vote Republican or Democrat?

CODY: [laughs] I think He'd be peaceful too. I think He'd just groove. He'd just look around and say, "Dang it man."

How to Make Your Own Bumper-Sticker Man Suit

For those of you interested in enjoying compelling, challenging, and uplifting conversation with people who aren't like you, I'd recommend donning a bumper-sticker suit and hitting the streets. I know that may sound like a daunting challenge to many, so I'd like to offer this simple, step-by-step guide to creating your own Bumper-Sticker Man Suit.

1. Purchase a plain, white painter's jumpsuit from your local hardware or paint store. I recommend a paper-based suit with the zipper in the front rather than the heavier and more expensive cotton jumpsuit.

2. Next, amass a collection of bumper stickers. Depending on your personal creative flair and design inclinations, you will need somewhere between twenty-five and forty bumper stickers. Be sure the slogans and messages cover a wide range of beliefs. As a helpful tip, be sure that you are personally offended by at least four of five bumper stickers. Remember, if your suit merely trumpets your personal belief system, you will miss out on stimulating and meaningful conversations.

3. I recommend attaching the bumper stickers and car emblems with superglue. This, of course, requires a high degree of care when placing each sticker. I tried duct tape, painters tape, and chewing gum, but

superglue really nailed it. I recommend pre-placing each sticker with an eye toward aesthetic and conceptual balance.

4.   All you need now are people to talk with. I found it easier to put on my bumper-sticker suit on location—riding in the car was fairly difficult and I was afraid the seatbelt would rip off the emblems. Busy public thoroughfares are an ideal place to meet and engage strangers in conversation. Try to stay in a wide-open area where people traveling in all directions can see your bumper-sticker suit. Avoid shouting profanities, sudden movements, and anything that may suggest you are selling something. Come up with a quick conversation starter like, "Can I ask you five quick questions for a documentary film I'm working on?" That worked for me, but you may want to personalize your approach.

1.   2.   3.   4.

One last thought: if your point of view leans toward the conservative, I would recommend a location in a large, urban area. This type of area probably has more people per square block likely to disagree with you—which is great for stereotype busting. I think you'll find this more challenging, interesting, and, if you're up for it, more beneficia

TAKE THE OFFICIAL
Lord, Save Us From Your
BUMPER-STICKER QUIZ

Review the following bumper stickers and circle the number that best suits your opinion. Check your score at the quiz's conclusion.

● ● ● ● ● ● ● ● ● ● ● ● ● ● ● ● ●

**CHRISTIAN
not close-minded**

1.   I will immediately place this sticker on my car. Dan, you can count on me.
2.   I concur with this message, but I will not put this sticker on my car.
3.   I'm a bit ambivalent about this one, Dan.
4.   I strongly disagree with this one, and I think I'm getting mad.
5.   Yes, I'm mad and I would physically remove this sticker from someone else's car.

1. I will immediately place this sticker on my car. Dan, you can count on me.
2. I concur with this message, but I will not put this sticker on my car.
3. I'm a bit ambivalent about this one, Dan.
4. I strongly disagree with this one, and I think I'm getting mad.
5. Yes, I'm mad and I would physically remove this sticker from someone else's car.

• • • • • • • • • • • • • • • • • • • •

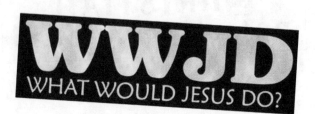

1. I will immediately place this sticker on my car. Dan, you can count on me.
2. I concur with this message, but I will not put this sticker on my car.
3. I'm a bit ambivalent about this one, Dan.
4. I strongly disagree with this one, and I think I'm getting mad.
5. Yes, I'm mad and I would physically remove this sticker from someone else's car.

1. I will immediately place this sticker on my car. Dan, you can count on me.
2. I concur with this message, but I will not put this sticker on my car.
3. I'm a bit ambivalent about this one, Dan.
4. I strongly disagree with this one, and I think I'm getting mad.
5. Yes, I'm mad and I would physically remove this sticker from someone else's car.

● ● ● ● ● ● ● ● ● ● ● ● ● ● ● ●

> I like your Christ.
> I do not like your Christians.
> They are so unlike your Christ.
> —Gandhi

1. I will immediately place this sticker on my car. Dan, you can count on me.
2. I concur with this message, but I will not put this sticker on my car.
3. I'm a bit ambivalent about this one, Dan.
4. I strongly disagree with this one, and I think I'm getting mad.
5. Yes, I'm mad and I would physically remove this sticker from someone else's car.

131

GOD BLESS THE WHOLE WORLD NO EXCEPTIONS

1. I will immediately place this sticker on my car. Dan, you can count on me.
2. I concur with this message, but I will not put this sticker on my car.
3. I'm a bit ambivalent about this one, Dan.
4. I strongly disagree with this one, and I think I'm getting mad.
5. Yes, I'm mad and I would physically remove this sticker from someone else's car.

• • • • • • • • • • • • • • • • • •

Evolution is just a theory— kind of like gravity!

1. I will immediately place this sticker on my car. Dan, you can count on me.
2. I concur with this message, but I will not put this sticker on my car.
3. I'm a bit ambivalent about this one, Dan.
4. I strongly disagree with this one, and I think I'm getting mad.
5. Yes, I'm mad and I would physically remove this sticker from someone else's car.

God Give Me The Strength To Deal With All The Idiots Who Cross My Path

1. I will immediately place this sticker on my car. Dan, you can count on me.
2. I concur with this message, but I will not put this sticker on my car.
3. I'm a bit ambivalent about this one, Dan.
4. I strongly disagree with this one, and I think I'm getting mad.
5. Yes, I'm mad and I would physically remove this sticker from someone else's car.

● ● ● ● ● ● ● ● ● ● ● ● ● ● ● ● ●

1. I will immediately place this sticker on my car. Dan, you can count on me.
2. I concur with this message, but I will not put this sticker on my car.
3. I'm a bit ambivalent about this one, Dan.
4. I strongly disagree with this one, and I think I'm getting mad.
5. Yes, I'm mad and I would physically remove this sticker from someone else's car.

IF RELIGIOUS GROUPS WANT TO GET INTO POLITICS, THEY SHOULD PAY TAXES

1. I will immediately place this sticker on my car. Dan, you can count on me.
2. I concur with this message, but I will not put this sticker on my car.
3. I'm a bit ambivalent about this one, Dan.
4. I strongly disagree with this one, and I think I'm getting mad.
5. Yes, I'm mad and I would physically remove this sticker from someone else's car.

1. I will immediately place this sticker on my car. Dan, you can count on me.
2. I concur with this message, but I will not put this sticker on my car.
3. I'm a bit ambivalent about this one, Dan.
4. I strongly disagree with this one, and I think I'm getting mad.
5. Yes, I'm mad and I would physically remove this sticker from someone else's car.

Who Would Jesus Bomb?

1. I will immediately place this sticker on my car. Dan, you can count on me.
2. I concur with this message, but I will not put this sticker on my car.
3. I'm a bit ambivalent about this one, Dan.
4. I strongly disagree with this one, and I think I'm getting mad.
5. Yes, I'm mad and I would physically remove this sticker from someone else's car.

● ● ● ● ● ● ● ● ● ● ● ● ● ● ● ● ●

1. I will immediately place this sticker on my car. Dan, you can count on me.
2. I concur with this message, but I will not put this sticker on my car.
3. I'm a bit ambivalent about this one, Dan.
4. I strongly disagree with this one, and I think I'm getting mad.
5. Yes, I'm mad and I would physically remove this sticker from someone else's car.

JESUS IS A LIBERAL

1. I will immediately place this sticker on my car. Dan, you can count on me.
2. I concur with this message, but I will not put this sticker on my car.
3. I'm a bit ambivalent about this one, Dan.
4. I strongly disagree with this one, and I think I'm getting mad.
5. Yes, I'm mad and I would physically remove this sticker from someone else's car.

● ● ● ● ● ● ● ● ● ● ● ● ● ● ● ● ● ●

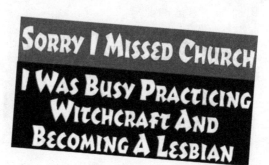

SORRY I MISSED CHURCH
I WAS BUSY PRACTICING WITCHCRAFT AND BECOMING A LESBIAN

1. I will immediately place this sticker on my car. Dan, you can count on me.
2. I concur with this message, but I will not put this sticker on my car.
3. I'm a bit ambivalent about this one, Dan.
4. I strongly disagree with this one, and I think I'm getting mad.
5. Yes, I'm mad and I would physically remove this sticker from someone else's car.

GOD WANTS SPIRITUAL FRUITS
NOT RELIGIOUS NUTS

1. I will immediately place this sticker on my car. Dan, you can count on me.
2. I concur with this message, but I will not put this sticker on my car.
3. I'm a bit ambivalent about this one, Dan.
4. I strongly disagree with this one, and I think I'm getting mad.
5. Yes, I'm mad and I would physically remove this sticker from someone else's car.

● ● ● ● ● ● ● ● ● ● ● ● ● ● ● ●

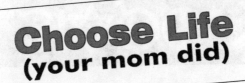

Choose Life
(your mom did)

1. I will immediately place this sticker on my car. Dan, you can count on me.
2. I concur with this message, but I will not put this sticker on my car.
3. I'm a bit ambivalent about this one, Dan.
4. I strongly disagree with this one, and I think I'm getting mad.
5. Yes, I'm mad and I would physically remove this sticker from someone else's car.

God created Adam & Eve
not Adam & Steve

1. I will immediately place this sticker on my car. Dan, you can count on me.
2. I concur with this message, but I will not put this sticker on my car.
3. I'm a bit ambivalent about this one, Dan.
4. I strongly disagree with this one, and I think I'm getting mad.
5. Yes, I'm mad and I would physically remove this sticker from someone else's car.

• • • • • • • • • • • • • • • •

1. I will immediately place this sticker on my car. Dan, you can count on me.
2. I concur with this message, but I will not put this sticker on my car.
3. I'm a bit ambivalent about this one, Dan.
4. I strongly disagree with this one, and I think I'm getting mad.
5. Yes, I'm mad and I would physically remove this sticker from someone else's car.

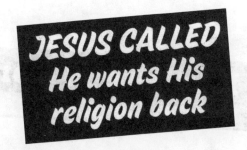

1. I will immediately place this sticker on my car. Dan, you can count on me.
2. I concur with this message, but I will not put this sticker on my car.
3. I'm a bit ambivalent about this one, Dan.
4. I strongly disagree with this one, and I think I'm getting mad.
5. Yes, I'm mad and I would physically remove this sticker from someone else's car.

● ● ● ● ● ● ● ● ● ● ● ● ● ● ● ● ● ● ●

Last time we mixed politics and religion people got burned at the stake

1. I will immediately place this sticker on my car. Dan, you can count on me.
2. I concur with this message, but I will not put this sticker on my car.
3. I'm a bit ambivalent about this one, Dan.
4. I strongly disagree with this one, and I think I'm getting mad.
5. Yes, I'm mad and I would physically remove this sticker from someone else's car

The Rapture is Coming
ARE YOU READY?

1. I will immediately place this sticker on my car. Dan, you can count on me.
2. I concur with this message, but I will not put this sticker on my car.
3. I'm a bit ambivalent about this one, Dan.
4. I strongly disagree with this one, and I think I'm getting mad.
5. Yes, I'm mad and I would physically remove this sticker from someone else's car.

The next time you think you're perfect try walking on water!

1. I will immediately place this sticker on my car. Dan, you can count on me.
2. I concur with this message, but I will not put this sticker on my car.
3. I'm a bit ambivalent about this one, Dan.
4. I strongly disagree with this one, and I think I'm getting mad.
5. Yes, I'm mad and I would physically remove this sticker from someone else's car.

Kind Words make good echoes

1. I will immediately place this sticker on my car. Dan, you can count on me.
2. I concur with this message, but I will not put this sticker on my car.
3. I'm a bit ambivalent about this one, Dan.
4. I strongly disagree with this one, and I think I'm getting mad.
5. Yes, I'm mad and I would physically remove this sticker from someone else's car.

● ● ● ● ● ● ● ● ● ● ● ● ● ● ● ● ●

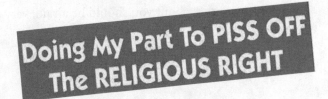

Doing My Part To PISS OFF The RELIGIOUS RIGHT

1. I will immediately place this sticker on my car. Dan, you can count on me.
2. I concur with this message, but I will not put this sticker on my car.
3. I'm a bit ambivalent about this one, Dan.
4. I strongly disagree with this one, and I think I'm getting mad.
5. Yes, I'm mad and I would physically remove this sticker from someone else's car.

HOW'D YOU DO?

● ● ● ● ● ● ● ● ● ● ● ● ● ● ● ● ● ●

Add up your points by counting the numbers you circled. So, one equals one point, two equals two points, and so forth.

25–45: Expand your horizons—a catchy bumper-sticker phrase is an inferior form of communication.

46–65: Relax, one or two bumper stickers can enhance the value of your car.

66–85: Step up and take a stand for something.

86–101: Settle down, settle down; we're just trying to start a conversation.

101–125: The people who care about you should be afraid, very afraid.

Chapter Eleven

beware the
HOLLYWOOD AGENDA

"Speak up! I can't hear you," the old woman shouts from the back of the crowd.

In the distance the man on the hill continues His address. "What's He saying?" she crows again.

A small, dirty man in front of the old woman turns to her, "I think He said, 'Blessed are the cheesemakers.'"

The old woman waves him away in disgust.

The nobleman's wife is confused, "Blessed are the cheesemakers? Whatever does that mean?"

With unfounded confidence the nobleman replies, "He doesn't literally mean cheesemakers."

"Oh?"

"He's referring to makers of any dairy products," the nobleman sniffs.

His wife shrugs and looks back to the man on the hill.

The goat farmer next to him strains to hear and takes his frustration out on the nobleman, "Hey Big Nose, keep it down I can't hear what He's saying."

"Don't call my husband Big Nose," protests the nobleman's wife.

"You shut up too," snaps the goat farmer.

"Don't tell my wife to shut up or I'll shut you up."

The small, dirty man turns around and glares, "*shhhhhhhh.*"

The goat farmer nods, "All right, let's listen up, there might be a part about blessed are the big noses"

The old woman, still unable to hear the man on the hill, gives up. "Let's go to the stoning," she says.

Here ends my paraphrase of the Sermon on the Mount as retold in Monty Python's *Life of Brian*, the rowdy, profane, R-rated comedy that mocks, not Christ, but His followers. When this movie debuted in 1979 it was condemned as blasphemous by the Church of England and banned in the Bible Belt of the U.S. by people who (wait for it) didn't even see it. I'm not saying this comedy is everyone's cup of tea, but I find this scene where Jesus preaches the beatitudes and the followers still can't get it right as strangely familiar and oddly encouraging. Just as Peter famously misses Christ's point repeatedly through the Gospels, here Python's first-century crowd stand at the feet of the Savior and misinterpret His words and treat each other poorly.

I was fifteen when *Life of Brian* opened, and though I was too young to see it (I didn't start sneaking into R-rated movies until I was sixteen), I sure heard the uproar rise from some of the faithful. I think the word *blasphemy* is such a powerful word that when it's thrown around it's like a hand grenade tossed into a room—everyone scatters. It's also a word open to interpretation. It reminds me of the famous Supreme Court definition of obscenity, "I'll know it when I see it." So when I finally saw the movie a few years later, I was totally shocked—totally shocked to find the blasphemy charge without merit. Oh sure, the movie is profane, contains nudity (of Brian no less, yuck!), and I understand if some folks feel a scene or two to be in poor taste (but taste is subjective). But blasphemous? No way. The film does do a masterful job of poking fun at organized religion, razzing an establishment that has allowed the faith to be diverted by fallible men. Actually, the complaints do make some sense as they came from the twentieth-century version of the institution Monty Python mocked. Rather than fess up to basic human failings that pervade the church, the leaders went after these humorous truth-tellers, calling for a boycott of this comedy. The protest struck me as funny and transparent. The church leaders didn't see how silly they looked yelling about a movie that humorously depicted a truth. Defensive much, fellas? In Jesus' time the religious institution didn't take too kindly to Him rocking the boat either.

And for those who are quick to revile Monty Python on religious grounds, a little trivia on *Life of Brian* for you: The project sprang to life when Eric Idle conceived a title, "Jesus Christ—Lust for Glory." Funny—but getting close to the line—but it's funny because it's so far from the truth, and in that juxtaposition lies the brilliance of Idle's concept. This spoof of first-century-Judean-messiah fever seemed a perfect follow-up to their hit King Arthur parody *Monty Python and the Holy Grail.* So the Pythons agreed to research the era and reconvene in a few weeks time to begin writing the script. But their research revealed something surprising that changed the shape of the project.

Interviewed for their biography, *The Python's on Python*, Eric Idle described his discovery:

We all went off and read the Bible, and I read the Dead Sea Scrolls . . . I think we realised (sic) at that point we couldn't make a film about Jesus Christ because he's not particularly funny and what he's saying isn't mockable, it's very decent stuff, you can't take the piss out of it. (*Python on Python*, pg. 279)

Fellow Python and *Life of Brian* director Terry Jones added:

The humour (sic) lay in somebody preaching and talking about peace and love, and then in people who spend the next 2,000 years killing and torturing each other because they can't quite decide how he said it. (*Python on Python*, pg. 280)

John Cleese, who portrays, Reg, the head of the Peoples Front of Judea in the film (or was it the Judean People's Front? Ha.), weighed in:

What is absurd is not the teachings of the founders of religion, it's what the followers subsequently make of it. And I was always astonished that people didn't get that. (*Python on Python*, pg. 280)

For some reason, I take great assurance from Monty Python's observation of my faith. I was fascinated that Monty Python's creators—who are bright, Cambridge educated, agnostic observers of this world—could look upon my faith and, basically, see what I see: Jesus delivered Truth. We only partially grasp it, but rather than admit our failings we build in excuses for our behavior and simplify His lessons until we have permission to be inert. We'd rather sit back and be right than admit how screwed up we are. We'd rather be right than make the effort to grow closer to Him. This is the lesson from *Life of Brian* as far as I'm concerned and, unfortunately, the people who banned and picketed the movie are the very people who could've gained some interesting insight had they bothered to see the film.

I was talking about *Life of Brian* with my friend Paul Metzger—author, theologian, and the founder of New Wine, New Wineskins, an organization dedicated to positive engagement with the culture. He reminded me, "Sometimes our worst enemies can be our best friends. *Life of Brian* is a movie a lot of Christians don't like, but it helps us see ourselves as we are and it can help us to be better."

I'm reminded of *Life of Brian* every time I hear some Christian railing on about how evil Hollywood is today. Clearly, there are film projects that do not reflect my values, and there are movies that literally may not include a redeeming quality—but those aren't the movies I hear Christians freaking out about. Remember the furor over Martin Scorsese's *The Last Temptation of Christ*? I can understand why people were upset that Jesus had a fantasy about sleeping with Mary Magdalene. But, I understood the filmmaker's point: if Jesus didn't have to choose between a barbaric death and living out a happy life with Mary down by the Sea of Galilee, *Then there'd be no sacrifice!!!* To me, this demonstrates how film can provoke thought, spark conversation, and ultimately lead to a deeper understanding. Again, I was disappointed that the Christians lost their minds, rather than engage and discuss the points involved. I don't think Scorsese was trying to offend people, but he tried to depict Jesus' humanity (a facet I don't think we fully appreciate). Scorsese was exploring the difficulty in God becoming man. We're oversimplifying, if we believe Jesus just showed up (virgin mother, manger—check), strolled through the pageant (raised the dead, rode a donkey—check), until it was time for the third-act climax at the Cross (betrayed with a kiss, rooster crowed three times, side pierced—check). Christ has to feel the pain, forgive us, and choose to absorb our sins in the ultimate sacrifice or the whole deal is a meaningless costume drama. Sure, I understand why people don't want to dig a little deeper—but must we condemn those who artistically explore the core questions of our faith?

Although twenty years have passed since *The Last Temptation of Christ,* it turns out we Christians still know how to shout down a movie. And thank goodness, because who knows what great crisis has been averted because we sounded the alarm on *The Da Vinci Code*? As it turns out, *The Da Vinci Code* didn't destroy America. Apparently, beleaguered Christians somehow managed to converse with their unbelieving friends about a summer popcorn movie without having to renounce their faith. The movie, starring Tom Hanks and based on Dan Brown's best-selling novel, ended up grossing 757 million dollars worldwide (more than 200 million dollars in the U.S.), which, in Hollywood lingo, is a "ginormous bank."

Yes, I'm aware the premise of the film asks me to believe that, among other things, Christ isn't divine. (I also saw *Hairspray* this summer and that film asks me to believe John Travolta is a woman.) Now, I understand there were some pastors who thought of this movie as a good hook to engage folks in a conversation about Jesus, and that seems reasonable, but then the hyperbole starting to flow. From various corners I heard phrases about *The Da Vinci Code* like "an assault on our faith," "lies aimed to destroy our faith," and "a blatant attack on the very foundation of Christianity"—which all are a tad overhyped and didn't ring true to me . . . especially when the pitch to buy the book debunking the code immediately followed these desperate cries.

What did we have here, a genuine warning to the faithful or a marketing opportunity? In July 2006, a month after the movie premiered, there were thirteen Da Vinci related titles in the Christian Booksellers Association's top fifty. Yes, people were interested in the topic and wanted to be a part of the conversation, but a little fearmongering never hurts business either.

Jimmy, soundman Terry, and I were in Colorado Springs the night that *The Da Vinci Code* opened. There had been reports that the film would be picketed, which would've been a great opportunity to get to the bottom of this, but nobody showed up to shout. I was actually encouraged by this and thought the whole thing would just fade away. So, Terry and I saw the film with a packed house and, you know, the movie was fine. My official review is *whatever*. The movie reminded me of *National Treasure* or even *Raiders of the Lost Ark*, not as much action, but the idea of taking a small touchstone of history and jumping off into a wild, exciting (sort of) adventure is a time-tested formula. After watching the movie, I felt comfortable *The Da Vinci Code* had as much to do with reality and was as big a threat to the church and my faith as *The Transformers* movie. If the church wanted to diffuse this issue and engage people with their questions about faith, we should've bought tickets and invited people to the movie and then out to coffee afterward.

I read an interesting Tom Hanks' quote in *Entertainment Weekly*:

> I think the movie may end up helping churches do their job. If they put up a sign saying: "This Wednesday we're discussing the gospel," 12 people show up. But if a sign says: "This Wednesday we're discussing *The Da Vinci Code*," 800 people show up. (July 2006)

After the screening in Colorado Springs, I interviewed a few people outside the theater. One young woman in her twenties, Erin, commented, "I'm not a Christian, but if a person went to this movie and it changed their faith, I guess I'd ask them, 'What was your faith in the first place?'" Bull's-eye.

Christianity is a faith strong enough to have survived Nero and the Vikings and the Dark Ages and Napoleon and Hitler and Communism . . . it'll survive Hollywood too.

Incidentally, I purchased a DVD debunking the book and Ron Howard's movie, which was produced by a major ministry. I wanted to be fair and listen to their concerns and try to understand where they were coming from. I tend to react quickly and am occasionally guilty of "popping-off," but I'm learning to be open to the idea I'm not right all the time. This seems like a healthy way to approach conflict, and, as an added bonus, I actually know what I'm talking about.

Anyway, the point I'd like to make is that this DVD cost me sixty bucks while the wide-screen, two-disc special edition of *The Da Vinci Code* only cost me $19.99. I may have purchased this at the "love gift" price, not at the retail price—and as an added bonus, I now receive regular telemarketing calls from this ministry. My efforts to engage the telemarketers in a theological discussion have been fruitless, partially because they barely speak my language and, unless I'm mistaken, the call is originating from the land where the Hindu and Muslim faiths are predominant.

Is this ministry or business? I'm fine if they call it business, but don't call it ministry and then do business. Nobody is buying that anyway, and it only creates something else for me to apologize for when I'm confronted by another annoyed, non-believing person.

I asked Tony Campolo about this phenomenon: "Is this just about money?"

Tony matter-of-factly responded, "Yes. I hate to say it, but yes. Some of these ministries need millions of dollars, maybe hundreds of millions of dollars, just to meet their operating expenses each year."

I'm not trying to beat up on anybody. I know people have questions, I know folks are concerned about the possible effects of things they see in the media, and I'm the very first person to say, "Let's talk about it, let's improve understanding." But how about if we create a guideline all of us can live with: if a ministry is simply providing followers with valuable, necessary information, fine—but if you made a boatload of money being outraged by *The Da Vinci Code*, then let's agree that if you keep that money you are never allowed to use the phrase "Hollywood agenda" ever again.

I wondered what others inside Hollywood (and much further up the ladder than me) thought of this conspiratorial notion.

I met with Mike Rich, a fellow believer, and veteran Hollywood screenwriter who has penned a slew of inspirational, heartwarming, soul-stirring films that dramatize the best of what we can be—films like *Finding Forrester*, *The Rookie*, *Radio*, and *The Nativity Story*.

DAN: How big of a surprise was *The Passion of the Christ*?

MIKE RICH: I remember hearing talk the week before the film opened and people were saying it might make a nice little ten-million-dollar opening. That next Monday we all picked up the trades, and it was clear this was a blockbuster.

DAN: Did Mel Gibson's film permanently change the Hollywood landscape?

MIKE: The impact of *The Passion* can't be overstated; it really opened Hollywood's eyes to an audience that is out there. Hollywood always wants you to appeal to what they call the Four Quadrants: young men, young women, older men, and older women. But when you consider 40 percent of the population will go to church on any given Sunday, if you are ignoring that figure it's basically like ignoring one gender.

DAN: *The Nativity Story* was the first religious-themed movie released by a major studio since *The Passion of the Christ.* Were you concerned how they would handle the film?

MIKE: When the elevator doors open and there are three posters on the wall and one is for *Snakes on a Plane*, the other is for *The Texas Chainsaw Massacre*, and the other is for *The Nativity Story*—it's a natural and obvious question. But I have to say New Line's level of support was consistent, steady, and very strong.

DAN: Yes, the very studio that is putting out this Christmas story also released *The Texas Chainsaw Massacre: The Beginning*, like we needed a fourth one, which was number one at the box office last weekend, by the way.

MIKE: [laughs] Exactly, exactly. Hollywood is a gun-shy industry. They're afraid of failure, and I think that's one of the reasons why you see so many movies that have a two or three or a four at the end of the title. You have studio executives who want to hang on to their jobs. The hardest thing to do is be bold. And it's the movie-going public that pays the penalty in the end because they don't get a good product.

DAN: The Religious Right, or the Christian Conservatives, or whatever label you want to use are fond of throwing around the phrase the "Hollywood agenda." What do you think they're talking about?

MIKE: Personally, I don't see it. *The Rookie* is an example of a film that was a live action, G-rated film. The projections were that we might make thirty, thirty-five million, and it made almost eighty million at the domestic box office. In my case, I've been success-ful at the box office . . . so when you come and you say, "We'd like to make *Radio*," which is another feel-good, family inspiring story, you tend to get a much warmer reception than if *The Rookie* had made fifteen or twenty million dollars.

DAN: So bottom line, this whole Hollywood thing has something to do with money?

MIKE: [laughs] It's always money. It's always money with Hollywood. I'd like to say there is a portion of their strategy that is based on putting quality films in their library, but I just don't see that very often anymore.

DAN: We can talk about the debatable moral merit of a *Texas Chainsaw Massacre*, but are those kinds of movies responsible for desensitization in our society? I'm trying to figure out where the objections—

MIKE: But you know what? When you make a movie like *Radio* or a movie like *The Rookie*, people come up to me and say, "Why doesn't Hollywood make more of those movies?" And you want to know what the answer is? Because people don't go to see them. "We see crap out there like *Jackass Two*; why does Hollywood keep making them?" Because people go see them. It's bottom-line driven. I have friends who say we live in a C-minus society. I don't want to believe them, but when I go to films with very little creative value, worthless pabulum, then I'll pick up the trades on Monday morning and see that it made forty-five mil-lion dollars at the box office. Is it frustrating for me and my friends who like to think we're making quality films? Absolutely, but that's the hard and fast truth, the reason that these movies get made is because they make money.

For a little perspective, here's a quick look at a box office scorecard: The two feel-good family sports films Mike scripted, *Radio* and *The Rookie*, grossed fifty-two million dollars and seventy-six million dollars, respectively. The combined budget for the two films was roughly sixty million dollars. So Mike actually did pretty well with both those films and 2006's *The Nativity Story* brought in almost thirty-eight million dollars and stands to be a perennial favorite on DVD. But compare that to the net profit of the horror series *Saw*. The first *Saw* film grossed fifty-two million dollars, which equaled *Radio*, but *Saw* was produced with a mere one million dollar budget. The next two *Saw* films, ingeniously titled *Saw II* and *Saw III*, grossed a combined three-hundred million dollars against a meager fifteen million dollar budget. That is profit of the highest order and therein lives the conspiracy: if a studio can make more money with a horror flick or any kind of flick, they'll do it. (As I write this in the summer of 2007, the remake of the teen slasher, uh, classic, *Halloween* was number one at the box office grossing nearly thirty-three million dollars in one weekend.)

When I sat with Al Franken at his Minneapolis radio studio, I asked him about the Hollywood agenda as well.

AL: The Hollywood agenda is to make money—making movies and television shows. That's the Hollywood agenda. I don't buy this whole "liberal Far-Left agenda by people like Steven Spielberg." He made *Schindler's List* and *Saving Private Ryan* whereas the Arnold Schwarzenegger's of the world make movies where people run around half-naked and shoot each other . . . and use steroids. There is a liberal community in LA; I, like many of those people and maybe some people in the liberal community in LA, are maybe not as knowledgeable of politics as they think they are, maybe they're a little bit arrogant because they've been very successful, they've made a lot of money so they're very smart. [Al laughs that laugh.]

DAN: Do you think the conservative Christians have anything to be upset about?

AL: Yeah, I don't mean to make it sound uncomplicated. It's too easy to dismiss those who think Hollywood is elitist and are lecturing to them. Things that offend me are, if you're watching a TV show, whether you're watching a comedy or a drama, where you end up knowing less about human beings after you've seen the show. Where it rewards you for not knowing how human beings work and makes you dumber. That actually offends me. I'm offended by a show that punishes you for knowing how people operate.

DAN: But is Hollywood, the *they*, not plotting away in a cigar-filled back room to offend Americans? That's not their goal?

AL: No. People in Hollywood, as a community, are probably more liberal. There are people who try to use their work to say things, to express themselves, which is such a terrible thing. [grins] And so maybe they're expressing ideas that are threatening to people, and they don't like that. Listen, I don't like a lot of what I see out there, but for totally different reasons. But, yeah, I can understand someone saying, "I don't want my kid to see that." Now, one of Hollywood's most successful industries is the porn industry. If you know anyone who works in the hotel industry they'll tell you that two-thirds of the films ordered in hotel rooms are porn. And who are they ordered by? They're ordered by businessmen, probably Republican businessmen [laughs]. But, you know, I don't hear that as the Hollywood agenda.

In 1988 I went to see a movie called *The Rapture*, starring a pre-*X-Files* David Duchovny and a ravishing Mimi Rogers. Thanks to my churching, I was a bit of a Rapture mythology expert and was interested to see how foolish and superstitious Hollywood would make me feel. Keep in mind, this film came out years before the *Left Behind* books and films came on the radar. Surprisingly, the film dealt very respectfully with faith and even played out the actual Rapture more realistically than I'd ever seen depicted. The film bore deep into the souls of the characters, their brokenness, their questions, and struggles about faith and, ultimately, dramatized the whole affair in a stirring, thought-provoking package. I was intrigued that the writer chose to explore this somewhat questionable facet of Christianity and dealt with it so respectfully. Personally, I think we overemphasize the whole Rapture thing. The popular theology only dates back to the 1800s and the biblical anchor is the confounding poem known as the Revelation of Jesus Christ. Trust me, this film packs a punch that makes *Left Behind* feel like a cartoonish, made-for-basic-cable movie.

The Rapture was written by Michael Tolkin, who would go on to write contemporary morality tales like *The Player* (Tim Robbins), *Changing Lanes* (Ben Affleck, Samuel L. Jackson), and *Deep Impact* (Robert Duvall, Morgan Freeman). I was pretty sure he'd have an interesting take on the culture wars and this whole Hollywood agenda thing.

I met with Tolkin in downtown Portland on a beautiful summer day while he was in the midst of a book tour promoting his new novel, *The Return of the Player*.

DAN: Your main characters always seem to be struggling in a moral area. We recognize these characters and struggle and squirm as their choices bury them. Is this how you see the lives we lead or is it hyped up for dramatic purposes?

MICHAEL: I don't believe in saints. Or at least what I understand to be the Christian notion of saints. I don't believe divinity and humanity mix; I think divinity and humanity are separate.

DAN: Why as a culture do we try to push complicated social issues into a black-and-white area, only to have these issues turn gray when we get to the particulars of our own circumstances?

MICHAEL: There's an interesting process going on in the world today, and I don't know how far back it goes, but in the process of religion or politics or ideology those with the most fanatical, hard-core, pious, fundamentalist interpretation of the Scriptures or of the tradition have the most authority within that tradition. So whether it's the most right- wing Christianity or the most exacting Orthodox Judaism or whether it's vegan to vegetarian, the most committed or most confident of the extreme position are the ones who control the debate and set the standards within each tradition. We are in a world right now with warring orthodoxies.

DAN: Does that power come from being able to convince the most people you are right?

MICHAEL: Those who offer the most confidence are the ones who have the most power, because as an animal we're more comfortable with guarantees than we are with, I don't want to say ambiguities or ambivalences because those are the common words . . . we want to avoid "wrestling." Israel means "those who wrestle with God," and as a Jew that's my tradition.

DAN: Let's talk about your film *The Rapture*. As a Christian, I remember seeing that film and being surprised how fair it was. Tell me about your inspiration and why that project?

MICHAEL: When I first got cable TV in the mideighties I started watching a lot of Christian television and I found that I really agreed with the basic diagnosis of the culture, that the culture was sick and insane and materialistic. I completely disagreed with the prescription, but I thought the sensitivity to what was wrong with the culture was right. *The Rapture* came out of what I thought was the most interesting conundrum of being born-again. It was interesting that, when the film came out, my Jewish gloss on mid-tribulationist evangelical eschatology turned into something that lapsed Catholics who were in twelve-step programs really liked. [laughs] And I'm not quite sure why.

DAN: I'm not surprised you had some interesting reactions to this film.

MICHAEL: There were sort of two camps. There were people who said, "This film is affirming the idea of God— it's horrible." There were people who said, "This film is affirming the idea of God—it's great." There were people who said, "This film is denying God—it's horrible." And there were people who said, "This film is denying God—it's great." [laughs] Mimi Rogers and I screened it for a group of Christians in Atlanta. I was asked some tough questions, but I had done my homework and I wasn't disrespectful of the sources. Even though I don't hide my Judaism at all, the film was taken seriously within that community.

DAN: I don't remember any protests against your movie.

MICHAEL: No. One of the people we screened it for had led the protests against *The Last Temptation of Christ,* and I think he found that the film was taking the issue seriously. Art allows you to push something into speculation, a situation that might occur in the real world, but the whole thing is a composition, it's all a supposition.

DAN: The movie creates such a realistic atmosphere, it's almost a twist ending when the Rapture actually does occur at the end.

MICHAEL: I'd never seen people walk out of a movie with forty-five seconds to go. There were some people who were so offended once the Rapture happens . . . they were so offended that I'd led them into a movie that says, "Okay, so God is real and all the Scripture is real and if it's real, then what?" They were so offended by the idea that I'd said, "God is real"—and these were people who were not religious or who are antireligious—it was curious to see. I was kind of tickled, you know . . . they'd already paid. [laughs]

DAN: In the years since your film, the *Left Behind* series has come out and sold sixty million books—

MICHAEL: Yeah, I know. I got there first but they got the money.

DAN: What is the fascination, or maybe a better word is *preoccupation*, with the end-times eschatology? Why are these books so popular?

MICHAEL: From what I've seen, the *Left Behind* series is definite in its depiction of good versus evil. That's not how I think. To me, what makes art or writing interesting is, you put people under extreme pressure and see what kind of problems they create for themselves and see how they handle those problems.

DAN: Lastly, I wanted to ask you about the Hollywood agenda.

MICHAEL: Hollywood is being scapegoated because it is vulnerable and ultimately weak. I don't really think there is any Hollywood agenda. Hollywood follows trends and fashions, and Hollywood's agenda is to entertain as many people as possible, to attract as broad an audience for every product it makes, and to make as much money out of that product as possible.

I think this money-first version of the Hollywood agenda is proven out when you consider the plethora of family films that have ruled the box office for years. When the Religious Right cries that Hollywood is corrupting our nation they are conveniently ignoring the true monster hits of the new millennium.

- *Shrek 2* ($436 million)
- *Spiderman* ($403 million)
- *The Return of the King* ($377 million)
- *Spiderman 2* ($373 million)
- *The Two Towers* ($340 million)
- *Spiderman 3* ($336 million)
- *Shrek the Third* ($321 million)
- *The Lord of the Rings* ($314 million)
- *The Chronicles of Narnia* ($291 million)
- *Shrek* ($267 million)
- *The Incredibles* ($261 million)
- *Toy Story 2* ($245 million)
- *Cars* ($244 million)
- *Ratatouille* ($199 million)

If you have seen any of these films, then you know themes of self-sacrifice, kindness, forgiveness, reconciliation, friendship, grace, justice, and redemption are at their heart. These virtues are at the core of Jesus' message—

isn't it interesting that movies exploring these themes in creative, visual, and interesting ways are the stories that capture the world's imagination?

Perhaps, the evils of Hollywood should be considered on a case-by-case basis rather than employing an overarching prejudice that may, in fact, serve some other agenda.

Former Senator Rick Santorum had a great insight on the Hollywood issue when he sat for an interview in fall 2006, shortly after his failed re-election bid.

I believe the conservatives have spent too much time complaining about what everybody else is doing to them, instead of going out there and engaging in ways that get the message out. Instead of just doing a Bible series, do feature-length films—not on the Bible, but on things that teach the same virtues in a way that people will want to watch them. People want to watch good entertainment; it's not just *The Nativity Story* or *The Passion of the Christ* that are important, I took my family to them, a lot of people did, but there are opportunities for us to tell stories in a lot of ways that pass positive messages on that reinforce the teachings of Christ without even mentioning His name.

As a Christian who has worked in Hollywood (to varying degrees of success), I am always a little annoyed by this notion of the Hollywood agenda. It's such a dismissive catchall that only fosters an us versus them mentality. And I have good news from the front that will come as a relief to some and, perhaps, a shock to others: Hollywood is full of people, Christians and non-Christians alike, who are ethical, passionate people who want to tell stories that elevate our world and enrich our lives. Yes, there are writers, producers, and actors who just want to get rich and buy big houses and fast cars, you know, kind of like lawyers, bankers, and real- estate developers.

I've met with many film executives to discuss the *Lord, Save Us From Your Followers* documentary. A few are Christians, but regardless of their religious background (or lack thereof), everybody seems to agree that the divisions in our culture feel wrong and they all want to do something to remedy this.

I recently sent a thank-you e-mail to an executive high up in one of the largest media conglomerates on the planet. In my note I teased him by feigning shock that there were decent people inside of this particularly monolithic media beast. Picking up on my tone, the executive playfully responded, "Yes . . . buried within the bowels of [insert name of giant film company here] are real, thoughtful, thinking people who relish the opportunity to make a difference. And . . . there's even more of us than the four you met in that conference room!"

A funny thing happens when you draw the dreaded beast out into the light . . . the beast turns out to be your own fear.

Chapter Twelve

the confessional BOOTH

We all know apologizing is hard, which is why most of us don't do it very much. But when I see it done, I'm always astounded by the results. One of my favorite examples is the confessional speech delivered by Pope John Paul II at the Vatican in March 2000. The Jubilee Apology took the occasion of two thousand years since Christ to assess the state of the Roman Catholic Church and to apologize for its shortcomings. The Pope's open, vulnerable position was unprecedented; there had never been an official statement approaching this level of contrition. His holiness apologized for all the forms of oppression that the Church had been guilty of from the Crusades and the Inquisition up through abetting the Nazis and the scandals involving priests.

Watching this speech I was moved, almost to tears—well, moved to moistness in the eyes for sure—and I recall being choked up a bit also. As the Pope spoke, I thought, *That's how we're supposed to do it.* There were many within the Church who begged the Pope not to give the Jubilee speech. There was the concern that if the Church admitted to wrongdoing, apologized for mistakes, that would somehow diminish the legacy or authority of the Church. Others still wondered why the Pope would apologize for wrongs committed a thousand years ago or more. But for me, the Pope's gesture was huge, and the goodwill generated from the apology echoed from that Jubilee homily.

Another confession I'm quite fond of took the baton from the Pope and carried it onto the most unreligious campus in America: Reed College in Portland, Oregon. Beautifully depicted in Donald Miller's delightful book *Blue Like Jazz*, this confession involved a couple of thirty-something dudes hanging out, auditing classes, and befriending the handful of young believers on a campus traditionally hostile to Christians. Donald's partner in crime for the aforementioned confession was a fun, odd, strikingly original kinda cat named Tony. Despite never writing a line of poetry in his life, Tony's penchant for pipe smoking and his goatee earned him the nickname "Tony the Beat Poet." Yeah, he just looked as if he ought to be a beat poet, so there you go. For the record, Tony has a last name, Kriz, but even he'll admit Tony Kriz doesn't ring like Tony the Beat Poet.

On the last weekend of April, the students of Reed deliver their theses and cut loose in an old school, nay, medieval way. In fact, this celebration of free expression and creative debauchery founded in 1968 is called Renn Fayre and, when clothes are involved, they are often of the Renaissance era. The dilemma for Donald and Tony Kriz was thus: How to participate in a non-condemnatory way with the Reed community during this celebration. The idea of a confessional booth was struck upon, but Tony threw in the hook—they would confess the sins of the church to those who would enter the booth.

"We sat down one day and asked ourselves, can we imagine being part of this weekend? Someone suggested a confession booth; I can't even remember who said it. After a moment I threw out the idea that we should confess to them. The idea kind of landed like a stone in the middle of the room—but it felt like a God idea," Tony said.

Yes, the Christian guys were going to confess to those mushroom-eating, liberal arts school pagans . . . and it would be fantastic.

I've spoken with Tony at length about his experience in the confession booth, and the thing that was the most amazing to me was the response from those to whom he and Don confessed. People let down their guard, opened up, and shared of themselves.

"People would walk in, and it's just a couple of dudes in their thirties, one of 'em losing his hair, saying, 'We're open to a genuine relationship even if it's just in this moment.' We spent a whole weekend in that booth, and I don't think the chair was ever empty. We'd talk for fifteen or twenty minutes, and then someone new would come in and sit down. 'Hi, welcome to the confession booth, if it's okay I'd like to begin.' And on it would go. We'd finish and the kid would say something like, 'That's the most f'ing beautiful thing I've ever heard.' Inevitably, there'd be a pause and then they'd start to tell me about their life, 'My dad used to beat the crap out of me when I was a kid.' And out would come these stories of pain, abuse, addiction . . ."

The entire context of the relationship was altered by one person willing to be humble, generous, and loving to another—whether the other "deserved" it or not. Just as with the Pope, remarkable aftershocks of this gesture have followed Donald and Tony on their many travels since that night at Reed College several years ago. Almost anyone who has read *Blue Like Jazz* will single this chapter out as particularly meaningful.

In watching the Pope's apology and talking with Tony Kriz about the Reed confessional booth, I was touched and provoked. Could I do something like that? What would that feel like? Whom do I owe an apology to? What would happen if every Christian in America, every Christian in the world, just up and apologized for something they'd done? I'm not talking about a forgotten atrocity from the Dark Ages that occurred on another continent; I'm talking about something I've actually done, something my church has done or is doing right now.

After a few minutes, my list of offenses grew long, and I grew depressed. Realizing this confession booth idea was a theatrical gesture, I thought, *What if I make it as difficult as possible?* This is where my God idea fell like a stone in the middle of the room: I got the distinct feeling I was to stage my own confessional booth at the Gay Pride Northwest festivities in Portland, Oregon. In truth, I didn't like the idea very much. And I don't think it was my idea—to be honest, the idea just appeared in my head and on my heart.

You see, Oregon is the least religious state in the union and also sports the highest concentration of lesbians per capita . . . yeah, when I was thinking it should be difficult I didn't mean like this—it definitely felt like God was piling it on a little.

I grabbed a beer with Tony Kriz and bounced my idea off him. I nursed my ale, he smoked his pipe, and we both thought long and hard. Tony agreed that there was much that the church had to apologize for to the homosexual community. He also pointed out the complications of the various issues around same-sex marriage. We discussed the Scripture specific to homosexuality and concluded that apologizing at Pride NW would be a great idea and a crazy one. There was a big difference between apologizing for the Crusades and communicating with someone where the party line was the oft confused and misinterpreted "I love you but I don't condone your lifestyle."

And, as we were filming a documentary, Tony didn't think the confession booth concept would work with little cameras just inches from the confessor and the "confessee." Tony didn't think anyone would actually come into the booth. I suspected the opposite. I thought that certain members of the gay community would be so shocked or fascinated to see a married Christian guy set up a confession booth at Gay Pride that curiosity would draw them inside. Lastly, I invited Tony to join me at Waterfront Park for the festivities. He took a long toke on his pipe, smiled thoughtfully, and shook his head no. Tony's confession booth experience at Reed had been a pure one, and repeating it wasn't part of his journey—this journey was mine.

"Besides," he smiled, "these people you're confessing to are going to ask you what you think about them, and you're going to have to tell them."

Yikes! I hadn't thought of it like that before. This wouldn't be like apologizing for helping the Nazis. I didn't help the Nazis. I don't know anyone who helped the Nazis.

But . . . I have been offended by homosexuals, I have made fun of them, I have mocked them, I have judged them, I have been disgusted by them, I have made myself feel superior to them, I have ignored their pain, I have contributed to their pain. I have forgotten that their sin is no worse than my sin. I have forgotten that any homosexual is just like me—a child of God. Aw, man, this was gonna sting, because I deserved whatever response I received. The more I thought about it the more I was convinced it was going to be an ugly day in the confessional.

Tony said something else that I took great encouragement from that helped focus and simplify my thinking. He said, "If we love somebody, we go out of our way to learn the best of who they are. And when you caricature someone you're saying, 'I don't care enough to actually know you.'"

In the days leading up to Pride NW, I thought of a friend I made in San Francisco while shooting for the *Lord, Save Us . . .* movie a few months prior—Sister Mary Timothy. Not knowing me from Adam, Sister Mary Timothy had agreed to be interviewed and, for two hours in a garden in the Castro, he shared his life with me. After taking a few minutes to adjust to his startling manifestation from Tim to Sister Mary Timothy, I came to enjoy the warmth, humor, and openness of this fellow child of God trying to find his way in this world.

I know this is obvious, but it's one thing to argue an issue in the abstract, it's another to discuss the issue with someone—to look into his face, truly listen to his voice. And sometimes I wonder what is more important to me and other Christians: spouting what we believe at someone or engaging that person? Would our spouting change, if we knew the rest of his story? That spring day with Sister Mary Timothy, I learned the rest of his story (see chapter 8). Sitting with Sister Mary Timothy was a riveting experience. Both of us listened, both of us were considerate, both of us were respectful, and both of us were allowed to be ourselves. He showed me that men who dress like nuns with KISS make-up needn't be feared—he wants the same thing I want and that is to be loved.

Now, the meeting with Sister Mary Timothy was one-on-one (well, I had a film crew with me, so it was four-to-one in my favor), and on a neutral site. Though technically in the Castro District, the garden was our own for the duration of the interview. On the other hand, the confession booth at Pride NW would not be on neutral territory. I was setting up shop in the middle of their party . . . something that might go over like a squeaky shoe in church. There would be thousands, maybe tens of thousands of gay people, and me (and my film crew so, four-to-ten thousand).

I even met with a local gay advocacy group who were pretty discouraging. Don't bother, they said. "Everybody just wants to party. I'd be surprised if anyone stops by your confessional." They even suggested setting up the booth in some other city. I wasn't clear if that suggestion was intended to be helpful or if they were giving me a not-so-subtle hint. I was disappointed they weren't more encouraging, but I suppose it did sound a little odd: "Hi, I'm a Christian; I want to set up a confessional booth at Gay Pride; sounds awesome, doesn't it?"

In fairness, when I told my own pastor what I had planned, he managed to force a smile and say, "Well, that should be controversial." I thought to myself, *If I do it properly it won't be controversial.* But I could understand the apprehension, when was the last time Christians and gays got together in public and avoided controversy?

Any second thoughts I was having were driven away the week before Gay Pride when I received an e-mail from a buddy who had been faxed a letter of warning from a local pastor. According to the e-mail, God was going to destroy Portland with a tsunami as an act of vengeance against the wickedness of the gays and those who tolerate them . . . at least according to some pastor's prophetic dream. The waves would crash, the rivers would rise, this group had a safe hilltop south of Portland all picked out and everything. If I were going to be killed by an act of God, I would at least be doing what I felt God had called me to do. Using my best Socratic reasoning, I figured if the prophetic pastor and I were both right, if we were both called to do this, I'd drown sharing God's love. If he was right and I was wrong, I'd skip the whole thing and watch the disaster on television. But if I was right and he was wrong, there was no way I would sit home and find out later that yet another prophet had misinterpreted God's message. No, I *had* to go through with it.

(Besides, if God calls you to do something, go—He probably knows something you don't know.)

We set the confessional booth up on a crisp morning in late June. As I watched the other booths being erected around me, I began to pray.

Usually, right before I screw something up, I'll remember to pray. I desperately wanted to undo the perception of Christians and of God that many of the people I was about to meet undoubtedly would hold. I wanted to beg people to listen to me: "We've been showing it wrong. Don't judge Jesus on my lame-o example. You've heard that part of the Bible where Jesus said, 'he who is without sin cast the first stone'? I think that part is important." I prayed for my words in the confession booth to be His words. I prayed I'd be able to see anyone who entered the booth as His child. I prayed I wouldn't do or say anything to damage His reputation. I prayed I would serve Him well.

Inside the Booth

A woman in her midforties with salt-and-pepper hair and a bright blue Hawaiian shirt entered the booth and sat opposite me. Her name was Gloria. We were separated only by a thin, translucent, burgundy-colored veil, which was our minor variation to the otherwise classic Catholic styling. I thought it was important that the people be able to see me while I confessed.

I swallowed hard but couldn't quite begin. Strangely, everything was how I had pictured it, but somehow when there is another human being expectantly searching your eyes it becomes startlingly real.

I had a quick flash of *Dan, what the hell were you thinking? You think you can come down here to their celebration and say, "Hi, I'm Dan, I'm a crummy person, and I'm sorry," and think that's going to mean something? You dumb, arrogant*—I actually thought about C. S. Lewis' *The Screwtape Letters* and wondered if the voice in my head was actually mine. But Gloria's round, smiling face immediately dissipated this last-second apprehension.

"This is my first time in a confessional, and so I thought it would be appropriate if I would confess," I managed with a nervous laugh.

"Okay, I appreciate that," she offered with smiling enthusiasm. *She was being awfully sweet to me. What a nice person*, I thought. She kept her eyes locked on to mine as I took a deep breath.

"I guess first I'd like to confess on behalf of the church, on behalf of the Christian faith, a church I love and am a part of, for the discrimination against you. We've really let you down, in light of what Jesus has taught us to do, which is to love one another and love our neighbors as ourselves. Our church hasn't done that and I haven't done that, not near as well as I can," I said in a steady voice.

"Oh!" she exclaimed, a bit surprised. I'm not sure if she knew what exactly I was doing, but she seemed to be getting more intrigued by the minute. I, on the other hand, was beginning to feel as if I had left my body. A peace began to come over me as I laid myself bare. I truly wanted this nice woman to know how sorry I felt.

"First, I want to apologize for that."

Gloria leaned forward, her brilliant smile again returning to her face, "Apology accepted."

"Thank you." I smiled back.

"I love you," she said. Tears started to form in my eyes and I'm not even sure why.

"I love you too," I replied with a giant smile that was controlling my face.

"Next, I'd like to apologize on behalf of the church for pretty much ignoring the AIDS crisis." I heard my smooth baritone roll on. I was quickly becoming a spectator to whatever God was going to do in this booth today. "When it first began almost thirty years ago, not only did we ignore this crisis, we labeled it a 'gay plague,' and we cast judgment and condemnation on people who were hurting and dying and losing friends to horrible deaths and I'm sorry. I want to apologize for that as well."

"Thank you," she said quietly, adding a gentle nod.

"I guess I'd also like to apologize for personally making jokes at the expense of homosexuals, for laughing at jokes aimed at gay people, and I want to apologize for participating in that poor behavior as well." I barely finished the sentence before my throat closed tight.

My new friend tilted her head, much like a nice auntie would, and smiled. "You are forgiven."

"Thank you," I squeaked.

"And lastly, I want to apologize to you for not living up to what Christ has taught me. I'm to show compassion, to show love, and I'm not to judge. I believe what the Bible says and it tells me, 'He who is without sin may cast the first stone' and my sins are numerous and that's not my job and I apologize for doing that. I apologize for all the people I've driven away from Jesus' love and grace though my bad example. I wanted to say I'm sorry for that too." A hot tear streamed down my cheek, even as my voice held steady.

"Absolved."

I nodded at my new friend, not expecting anything, but simply grateful she was willing to hear me out.

But Gloria leaned closer, "I want to thank you for speaking this to me. I appreciate hearing these words. It does a lot to heal my heart. I was just thinking the same thing, *How could Jesus' followers hate so much?* So it's lovely to hear this from you and know that all of you don't hate us."

"No, no, all of us don't, we're just not doing as good a job as we should. I think in some cases we allow ourselves to be ruled by fear instead of being guided by faith—"

"And love," she interjected.

"And love. Jesus is pretty radical. He asks a lot of us and expects a lot of us," I offered.

"And He embraces everybody."

"The thing that's particularly troubling to me is that when we engage with people we may not agree with, we seem to forget the essentials, love one another," I offered.

"That is very elemental," she agreed. "You know, I have to be honest

Dan, one of the things that kept me from being a Christian was being treated so poorly by Christians. And though I'm not a Christian, I appreciate Christ's teachings. I appreciate the words you're saying to me today, and I love you for it."

"Thank you. And if I could say, don't judge Christ by me or others like me, judge it by Him—He's the only one who got it right anyway." I shrugged.

Gloria burst out laughing, "It's true, isn't it?" She beamed at me and blew me a kiss, "Thank you very much."

"Thank you for participating. God bless you," I stood as I spoke.

"God bless you."

She stood and parted the velvet curtain and stepped out of the confessional. I can still hear her as she exclaimed, "That was so powerful!" to one of her friends outside. I sat on the chair, staring at the veil and thanked God for being with me. It is a very intense thing to open up to a complete stranger. But there is a freedom in not holding on to this old baggage; there is a peace in being transparent. I was also very grateful that Gloria had chosen to accept my apology. Frankly, I was a little surprised and fascinated that she had. It almost felt as if she had been waiting for someone to say something like this to her. I didn't expect the whole day to go this well, but at least the first confession had gone well. I was ready if anyone else was willing.

About forty seconds later a young man named Jovan entered, wearing a bandanna on his head and sporting green cat eyeglasses.

He listened quietly and attentively while I gave the apology, again in three parts: apologizing for my church, specifically for our failings regarding the AIDS crisis, and finally for my own sins. Jovan nodded tightly a couple of times but was absolutely silent.

After I finished there was a pause, "Thank you, I appreciate you coming in."

He nodded again, but didn't move, "Awesome," he whispers and then smiled. He still didn't move.

Sensing a conversation, I obliged, "Have you ever been in a confession booth before?"

He opened his mouth to speak, but nothing comes out. He nodded again.

I continued in a casual tone, "Have you experienced unkindness and judgment at the hands of people who say they love Jesus?"

"Yeah, I grew up in Wyoming," Jovan said, "and it's pretty Podunk and really scary. I have stab wounds . . ." His surprisingly deep voice trailed off.

I wasn't sure I heard him right, so I just waited for him to continue.

"I'm a recovering heroin addict."

No, he definitely said "stab". "Did you say stab wounds'?"

Jovan nodded, "Yeah, I've been gay bashed a number of times."

Though I've heard of gay bashing, Jovan was actually the first person I'd met who had suffered through something like that.

He continued, "So it's very important for me to hear what you're saying. And actually I believe in Jesus."

"I'm sorry you had to go through something like that," I offered. "Did that happen a long time ago?"

"Yeah, it was, and I'm a lot stronger because of it. Now I do a lot of non-profit work. So things are better." He smiled.

"I'm glad."

"What's your name again?" Jovan asked as he stood up and took my hand.

"Dan."

"Thanks, Dan."

I leaned around the veil to shake his hand properly and saw that his eyes were wet. *Glad I am not the only one crying in here.*

I stepped out of the booth to see if there would be any more confessions given, and saw there was a crowd of people waiting. My producer buddy, Jon, who was running this shoot for me, was up to his elbows in talent releases and curious people. Jimmy, his camera on his shoulder, circled the booth picking up shots at the busy festival. As happens with God ideas they become what they are supposed to become, not what you think they are going to become.

To put it mildly, our wooden confessional booth was not like the other booths on the thoroughfare at Pride NW. We were the only booth with a red velvet curtain for a door, a wooden cross overhead, and, as an added bonus, a crucifix and a small statue of the Mother Mary perched on the front façade. And yet this strange set prompted curiosity instead of anger.

Kimberly, a sturdy woman in a blue polo shirt, probably about my age, entered the booth. The first moment or two in the booth must have been a little strange, but her serious expression was replaced with a slight smile as I began my confession. With each person I found the words to the confession tumble out of my mouth differently—seemingly with minimal participation from me, if that makes sense. My apology to Kimberly was personal and ended this way:

DAN: I want to apologize for allowing fear to drive me, instead of faith. For being put off and offended in ways that Jesus would not want me to be, in ways that are selfish and hurtful to others, when Jesus is really clear about how He asks for me to love one another. I apologize for not doing that, for not loving you the way that I should.

KIMBERLY: I accept your apology and want to say thank you for speaking up. I'm tired of people not speaking up anymore. I'm tired of people corrupting the church and claiming that they know God when they carry banners that say "God Hates Fags," because God doesn't hate anybody. I'm tired that we've been quiet for so long, because I'm a Christian. People of faith need to stand up and say, "Jesus came to save us, all of us—not a select few." The conservatives in this country don't get to set the agenda for God. So I want to thank you for speaking up and speaking out.

DAN: To presume to know the heart of God is tricky business. He gives us His Word to work from but for a political agenda to say being a homosexual is a sin of greater magnitude than my selfishness or my pride or my arrogance or my lust or my stealing—If we're going to single out people we better not forget that verse, "He who is without sin cast the first stone." I don't think Jesus said that on a whim.

KIMBERLY: I think what's so frustrating right now—and I read the Scriptures—is that it says we are called to take care of the poor, the widow, and the orphan. That's our responsibility. And we have people making the greatest profits in the history of the world and our government is allowing them to do that. Taxes are being cut, and the poor are not being helped. We're not even doing the most basic message of God, the most basic message of Jesus; instead we're beating up other people. And where is Christ in the message? I don't hear Christ in the message anymore. We are called to be children of God as much as anyone else, and it's about inclusion and we understand that message.

DAN: Jesus goes out of His way to demonstrate how to do it. He didn't hang with the rich people or the politicians; He went to the marginalized. I think there's a somewhat obvious lesson in there about how we're supposed to treat each other.

KIMBERLY: And Jesus was a radical. He not only advocated a way of loving each other and treating each other better, but He also advocated a way of confronting one another when things are not right; when there's no justice, when there's no love. Jesus confronted the people and said, "It's not okay." I don't advocate violence; I advocate confronting people the way Jesus showed us through the power of love and the power of speaking up and out.

DAN: *Radical* is a good word. I have to laugh at the *South Park* cartoon where Jesus returns for the Second Coming and nobody recognizes Him so He has to resort to hosting a cable access show called *Jesus and Pals.*

KIMBERLY: I love that. Did you see the one where *Jesus and Pals* gets into a ratings battle with the hunting and killing show on the other channel? [laughs] It was so bad and so funny and so real.

DAN: Yeah, it's shocking where we're finding little pockets of truth these days. [laughs] Well, thank you for accepting my apology, Kimberly. It was great to meet you.

KIMBERLY: Thank you again for your work.

With each successive person, it became clear that these folks didn't want to fight, they wanted to understand. They wanted to know, "What was up with the Christians?" And, like me, they wanted to connect.

My next guest was Susan: short red hair, forties, suede jacket open over a T-shirt. She was the first of several ex-Catholics to enter my confession booth. After laughing, "All right, I've been in one of these before," Susan sat quite still and listened to my apology.

SUSAN: You know what EGO means? Edging God Out. [laughs] We get caught up in our own egos; we have a tendency to not do God's will. I think what we're put here on earth to do is to help one another, but we can get lost in our own stuff and forget that. Times are so stressful in the world today, it's a wonder people even take time to talk to one another.

DAN: Yeah, God's pretty clear—how do we show Him we love Him? Love each other.

SUSAN: It's hard to know what God's will is for us 'cause our will kind of likes to run the show. At least I'm speaking for myself; maybe there are others who could say the same thing. When I talk I like talking about myself and not include a group, but it's hard because you want to be in a group, you want to be liked and I think a lot of us search for that, looking for a place to belong but sometimes you just feel like, *I don't belong anywhere."* [Susan raises her palms to the sky and looks up.]

DAN: Have you gone to church? Do you go to church?

SUSAN: I've gone to Unity in Seattle. I grew up Catholic, very guilt based. I always said I was going to die and go to purgatory and just wait there for judgment day.

DAN: How did the church make you feel, growing up?

SUSAN: I ran from it and started smoking pot all the time. I'd go to church then sneak out and smoke, pretending I'd heard the service, "Monsignor Brett said this . . ." It was very guilt based, very sad. They weren't emotionally available, really, to what kids go through, to what I went through as a kid. I lost my best friend at thirteen, and no one was there.

DAN: You'd hope the Christian faith would be pretty good at compassion, considering Jesus' example.

SUSAN: It's a sad thing. I feel heavy just being in this little booth.

DAN: When you were a kid, you'd go to confession?

SUSAN: Bless-me-father-for-I-have-sinned-it's-been-about-a-month-since-my-last-confession-these-are-my-sins. [Susan rattles

176

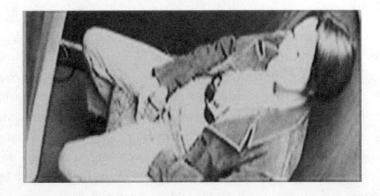

off the confession as if it were one long word.] Yeah, I did that a couple times, you know. I can make fun of it today. But even thinking back, where they slide that thing open but you're not supposed to really see them but they know who the hell you are. [She sighs deeply as the memory fades.] I can't even remember what I confessed.

DAN: I heard a great Dennis Miller joke the other day. He grew up Catholic as well and he talks about sitting down in the confession booth and saying to the priest, "You first."

SUSAN: Yeah, no kidding.

DAN: What have you noticed lately about Christians at large? There are quite a few hot-buttons flying around.

SUSAN: They're p***** off about *The Da Vinci Code.* I think Jesus lives in all of us so in that way the bloodline has gone forward. God is in all of us, and God means "Good Orderly Direction."

DAN: [laughs] Where do you get these acronyms?

SUSAN: Alcoholics Anonymous. Eighteen years clean and sober.

DAN: Congratulations and thanks again for accepting my apologies.

SUSAN: Thank you.

As the day went on I would confess to twenty-four people and each time a conversation would spring forth. It was really amazing to see the power of the apology, how it leveled the playing field—we were all just children of God sitting down for a chat. I must say I was repeatedly taken aback at the generosity of those entering the booth, their willingness to allow me to confess, to listen politely and patiently. I was also moved by their decision to share their stories with me. I had personal conversations with many people over their deepest, most seminal hurts: a man who was fired from his job for being gay, a twenty-something whose fundamentalist parents made him feel unloved by sending him to gay boot camp as a teen, a thirty-something woman who had been singled out by a political action group and labeled the "head of the Sodomite lobby," a teen lesbian who was kicked out of the parents' home when she was seventeen when she came out to them. When you meet the people, hear their voices, see their eyes, it changes everything—the conversation is no longer a political abstract; it's now about a person who is hurting. It's too easy to say, "You hurt because you've made the wrong choice. It's your own damn fault." If that's done without the context of a relationship (as it usually is), it simply sounds like "I hate you."

George, a sweet little man who I'd place in his mid-fifties, sat down in the booth, and I could instantly tell he was on "high alert." He was dressed in traditional Tibetan Monk attire, my first clue, and his bespectacled eyes darted around the booth.

"Do you have the same thing you say every time?" he asked.

"More or less, I feel there are some basic—"

"You can change it. You're not reading a script," he probed.

"Oh, no, no" I stammered. Then I noticed George was laughing. He was gently putting me on, and I hadn't realized it. As you can imagine, I was trying to be sensitive and aware not to inadvertently offend someone and didn't have my humor at the ready. *I get it. George is a funny guy. Okay, I can play that too. But no, this is from my heart.* "I feel pain from my own shortcomings and the pain we've caused others. So, I guess to start from the start, I want to apologize . . ." and I proceeded through the first portion of the apology. George watched with an empathetic look on his face and my voice choked up a little as I completed my first thought.

George bowed graciously and even through the veil I could see he was becoming emotional.

I proceeded with my second apology: the part about ignoring the AIDS crisis. As I was saying this to George, I could only imagine how different his life and many other lives would've been if the church had been there to love and help with no questions asked. I thought about Kaye Warren's AIDS hospice work now and as part of the training volunteers are told, "Don't ask how they became sick. You'd never ask someone suffering from heart disease if they'd eaten a lot of red meat."

George nodded through the last half of the AIDS apology. When I finish he simply said, "You're right."

Again, throughout my personal apology, George nodded in recognition as the various details of my weakness hit home. "I haven't loved my brothers and sisters as myself; I don't do a good enough job at that and as a result have absolutely misrepresented Jesus and His grace and truth and love in this world, and I apologize for that. I've distorted His vision and I ask that you'd forgive me for those things too."

We sat and looked at each other for a moment. George started to speak, but fought back tears, "I don't know what to say." He collected himself then continued, "I'm not in a position to forgive."

"I know the judgment you've felt has caused hurt, and I'm embarrassed by that because that judgment is out of my jurisdiction. I'm as big a sinner as they come and that's the Maker's territory." I shrugged.

"Me too. I apologize too." George looked down at the ground and took a moment to compose himself. "I don't know what I'm suppose to say. You're apology about the AIDS thing really kinda touches me." His voice cracked and wavered. "Uh, I wish there were more people who had that feeling early on, having lost so many friends." His voice trailed off to a whisper. "Sorry."

"I know. If in that time and space the church would've reached out with Christ's compassion it could've changed the world. We called it a plague when it was an opportunity to show God how much we loved Him and we failed. I hope we're doing better now."

George removed his wire-framed glasses and wiped the tears from his eyes, "I'm sorry."

"No, please, George, it's fine." Now I was the one who was not sure what to say. "In the way some Christians have stereotyped gay people, I know Christians are also stereotyped. I'm just trying to put the focus on Jesus and the red letters in the Bible and ask that our faith be judged on Him and not me or my compadres that carry signs." I laughed.

George smiled too. "We have the same issue in Buddhism. It's hard, I think, for people who want to be spiritual. When people visit our temple I tell them, 'There's a lot of support out there for being a jerk, but there's not a lot support out there for being a good person.'" He paused again, looking downward. "It's very touching, the apology, but I'm not sure I'm worthy of receiving the apology." His face turned up to meet mine, "That's . . . that's the hard thing to face."

I wanted to hear the rest of his thought and clumsily pushed on, "What do you mean by that?"

"Well, I'm as guilty as the next person," he said, his voice rising to emphasize his point. "So I'm not necessarily the person worthy of receiving the apology. I know none of us are perfect, but hopefully we're all trying to do the best we can." Again, we sat for another moment in silence. "It's interesting to sit in here and listen to you apologize."

"I'm continually amazed by the things that don't make sense in this world, the things that don't add up, like grace and forgiveness and an apology. There seems to be this unknown quality, this transformative power in it," I said with that giant smile plastered across my face.

"Yeah, coming in here, the experience inside is a lot different than the anticipated experience when you're outside," George said, smiling back. "Listening to someone apologize, whom I assume and believe is sincere in their apology, is . . . and if we're dealing specifically with Christianity, just the hurts I've received personally from Christianity, and I know other people have received as well—it's been frustrating. That's what led me away from Christianity thirty-nine years ago. I didn't see anything in Christianity that welcomed me. I know that all Christians aren't that way but you're the first Christian I've ever had apologize to me." George's laugh bubbled up as he released what he'd been carrying for some time. His voice suddenly quieted. "It's touching, it's touching for you to say that to me."

"Thank you for being open enough to give me the opportunity," I added.

"Well thank you for doing this," George bowed again and laughed, a little dazed as he exited the booth, "Yeah, that was weird. Not weird in a bad way, weirdly powerful. Not what I expected."

I knew exactly what George meant. Sitting in that booth, confessing my sins to a group who is used to being picketed by Christians brought forth this otherworldly combination of euphoria/sorrow, relief/pain, intimacy/distance, grace/affliction—but I guess none of those can exist without their counterpart anyway. You know what it felt like? *Being real.* Let's just cut the crap and focus on what's important for a minute and see if we can understand each other, find our common ground, focus on what is important. I don't know how it sounds to you or looks from the outside, but the feeling was a good feeling.

I left Waterfront Park that evening emotionally drained. I was hopeful, but I had touched so much sadness that I cried in my car for a half-hour and just begged Jesus to present Himself to my new friends, to relieve them of any pain, and to guide them home to Him. I was so sad that, in many cases, we Christians had chased them away. I wept for them, and wept for all of us who had done this damage.

The day after my confession, the Gay Pride parade was held. And even though it was Father's Day and I was out with my family, I had this nagging inclination to circle the parade route just to be sure there weren't any Christians along the way with protest signs. I found myself defensive for the people I had shared time with the day before. The people I had shared my heart with, and they with me. The people who were curious about why a

Christian would try so hard to let them know that God is love. I suppose some may have considered me an anomaly, but still, if the Christians along the parade route were to call out "I love you and God loves you!" then maybe my new friends would start to think something was up.

Strangely or understandably, I had a few heated conversations with Christians who questioned the value of these engagements. Their position was I had an obligation to tell them the truth and to try to save them from hell. I would agree on the end goal and disagree on the means. In screen-writing there is an old maxim, "Show me, don't tell me." Demonstrating love, sacrificing for one another, speaks much more loudly than simply delivering empty platitudes. People can tell the difference anyway.

Besides, I feel like we can go on all day about the whole "gay issue," but what I'm talking about is a people issue, a "we're all God's children issue," and since I'm a believer, a "what would Jesus do" issue. This isn't about whether the Gay Pride parade is outlandish or offensive. This is about obedience and humility—and I'm not talking about the gay people, I'm talking about the Christians. Before you scrawl a Bible verse on a sign and wave it in someone's face, I would ask you to take that someone to dinner. Or volunteer in an AIDS hospice for a month. Or take in a musical with someone you think is going to spend eternity in a "lake of fire." I guess I'm asking you (and reminding myself) to try to see everyone the way God sees them, and if that means looking past glitter makeup, falsies, and platform shoes, then *do it*! Yeah, I know it's easier to stand on a parade route with your friends being obnoxious and self-righteous, but, in case you haven't noticed—*that doesn't work*. The only thing strident arrogance is good for is hardening hearts, fostering resentment, and creating animosity. I'm still looking for the verse where God instructs us to create that—if you find it, e-mail it to me, will ya?

Tony Campolo tells a moving story of an incident from his youth in the *Lord, Save Us From Your Followers* film. This heartbreaking anecdote always puts this issue in perspective for me.

"When I [Tony] was in high school there was this boy named Roger, and he was outted—a gay kid, and his homosexual orientation became known. West Philadelphia High was a huge and tough inner-city school.

You can imagine what we did to this kid some fifty years ago when ignorance prevailed in this issue . . .

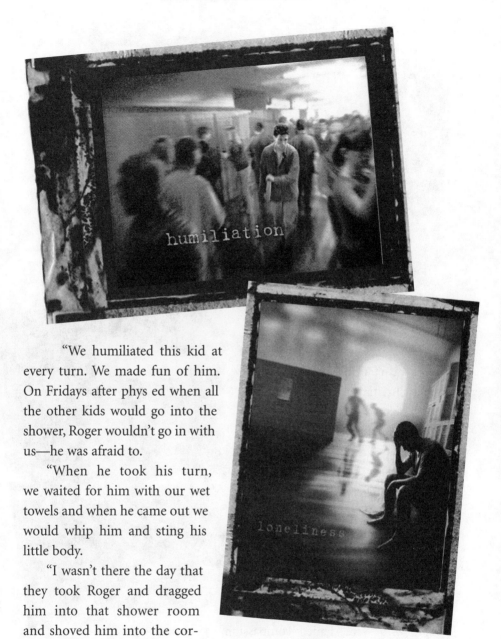

"We humiliated this kid at every turn. We made fun of him. On Fridays after phys ed when all the other kids would go into the shower, Roger wouldn't go in with us—he was afraid to.

"When he took his turn, we waited for him with our wet towels and when he came out we would whip him and sting his little body.

"I wasn't there the day that they took Roger and dragged him into that shower room and shoved him into the corner. And while he yelled and screamed for mercy five guys urinated all over him. I wasn't there when that happened.

"He went home. He went to bed at about ten o'clock. They say it was about two o'clock in the morning when Roger went into the basement of his

mercy

despair

house and he hung himself. And I knew I wasn't a Christian because if I were a Christian I would have been Roger's friend. You don't have to legitimate someone's lifestyle in order to love that person, to be brother or sister to that person and then stand up for that person."

My heart broke over and over again on the day I begged complete strangers to forgive me for the hurt I'd caused and to share my empathy for the hurt they'd sustained. My heart broke for people who were denied compassion, who received judgment instead of tenderness, who were shouted at instead of listened to, who were pushed away instead of held. It was moving for me to have people share their stories, their hurts with me. In those moments it was so clear to see how we are all the same: human beings just trying to find our way home.

You want one more confession? I've hurt more people than just the gays. Yeah, news flash, right? I could take this confession booth on tour and apologize to *almost* everyone I've ever met . . . okay, fine, *everyone*. Being honest with myself and my Lord isn't too much fun sometimes, but when I let my guard down with Him, release my ego, I'm actually allowing Him to heal me. That's the amazing part in this apology business. When you finally decide to release whatever

you're holding, when you let go of the hate, hurt, anger, resentment, whatever, something wonderful rushes in to fill that void . . . God's love. That's a pretty good trade-off, don't you think?

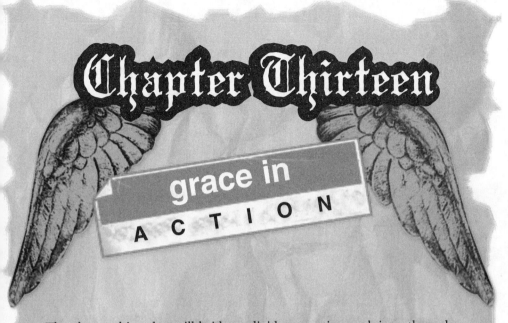

Chapter Thirteen

grace in ACTION

There's one thing that will bridge a divide every time: valuing others above ourselves. Putting another's need above your own, that's the secret sauce. That's why Mother Teresa was such a superstar—all she did was put the needs of others above herself. The advertising world is built on selling the notion of "you better get yours, you deserve it," but, oh man, we've missed it. We're so in love with our own comfort we can't see anyone else. We've been hypnotized. This is why when we do see those people sacrificing for others, we simply figure they're freaks or destined for sainthood. But is it fair to dismiss them as the oddity when, actually, they're the only ones who get it? If they're doing it properly but are in the minority, they're still the ideal, right? It's funny, I trust the motives of those who are helping others with no chance of reward or personal gain. Only then do I believe they're actually doing it, for the other person, and if that's why they're doing it, then I'm with them.

The difference between trying to win an argument with someone and demonstrating love is the difference in the by-products: animosity or meeting needs.

If you show people something real, something beautiful, they will *want* to talk. Why is the gospel of love dividing America? Because people are tired of hearing about love and *not* seeing enough of us show it. It's time to *do*. And by do, I don't mean take action for our cause; I mean selflessly assist someone in need, love one another, show me don't tell me. People can't help but respond to the authentic. Truth doesn't have to shout, "Hey all you losers look at me, I'm Truth and you're not!" No, when Truth walks in the room, everybody simply stands up.

Enter Sheila Hamilton, a veteran media professional whom I first met briefly in a Seattle elevator in 1991 at the Northwest Region Emmy Awards. We had both entered the elevator, but neither of us could push the buttons for our respective floors because we were each holding two Emmys. Sheila said something funny like, "Somebody else is going to have to hit the button because I'm not letting go of these." (Now that I think about it, I could've said the joke, but since I'm writing this book this is how I choose to remember it.)

If you flip on the radio during afternoon drive-time in "godless Portland" (you remember the playful moniker given to us by the Take Back America crowd), you'll hear Sheila, who is now the news director and afternoon show co-host at rock station KINK-FM. I had originally contacted Sheila to participate on the Liberal Media Elite team in our culture wars game show, but a scheduling mistake botched that. But, as these things go, Sheila would take a trip to Africa and her experience would lead me to as compelling an interview as I would conduct for the movie.

A little backstory: in 2006, Sheila traveled to Ethiopia with Christian relief organization World Vision in an effort to help find sponsorship for four hundred AIDS orphans.

SHEILA: Apparently World Vision has partnered with Christian radio for drives like this before but never with a secular radio station, which I found both fascinating and appalling. Like people who listen to secular radio wouldn't be interested, and all this time I'd been interested in Africa and was waiting for someone to ask.

DAN: You had? When had you become interested in Africa?

SHEILA: I saw Bono at the World Affairs Council give a speech about "how it's our moral time to do something about Africa." I hadn't even paid attention to Africa; it's so depressing and overwhelming. So Bono said he was going to start this ONE organization, and so I kinda got interested in this whole issue of poverty and AIDS and I joined. Back then there was nothing else to do. I thought, *Shouldn't they be asking us to do something besides just give our signature?* So I signed on to the Clinton AIDS Foundation, and they actually asked for money. But I still felt so separate from really understanding what's happening and really being able to do something. So that was where I was when my program director called and said, "How would you like to go to Africa?" You know, I kinda think things happen for a reason. I said, "I'd love to." World Vision wanted to show us, a secular radio station, for the first time their work going on in Africa. I said, "I would love to go . . . I have some reservations."

DAN: Let's talk about those reservations, what were you concerned about? What did you expect to see?

SHEILA: I had heard about World Vision, probably through their TV commercials, and I understood they were a Christian organization. My greatest fear was that I would go into these camps where children were dying, and I would see Christians proselytizing. It's a traditional Muslim country with Christianity at about 45 percent, and I was afraid this would cause a lot of chaos. But World Vision assured me that what they're doing in Ethiopia is providing relief; they're getting water, digging wells, and improving agriculture. And that if by doing those actions people see their work and want to find out more about who they are and what they believe, then they're open to that. So that set my mind at ease.

DAN: What did you actually see when you got there?

SHEILA: It's funny. One of the first things I noticed was the Muslim call to prayers, and I found myself thinking, *Where's the Christian equivalent?* Mostly we saw World Vision's good deeds: we saw them delivering bags of seeds, digging wells, bringing amazing farming capacity to people who had never in their lives seen anything beyond a hoe. And most of these people were Ethiopians, and that was another selling point for me. World Vision doesn't go in there with a bunch of white people and say, "You must believe before we feed you." They hire Ethiopians and teach them how to better their own lives, and I was so impressed.

DAN: Do you find there's a difference between demonstrating love for your brother as opposed to simply telling him?

SHEILA: I'm very leery of the guys coming to your door telling you about the Book. It's always just felt like I'm being knocked over the head. But when I personally see people actually living the Word of Christ I'm moved to tears. Like to see these women holding those babies who are ravaged by AIDS, and knowing that they've already helped bury the mother and the father and they're doing that as the work of Christ. It makes me want to find out more about Christianity. I really had such an eye-opening experience to the whole world of Christianity because of what we went through there.

DAN: It's a remarkable thing, and it's probably not a coincidence, to see Muslims and Christians living together without strife—

SHEILA: Not at all. Living together side by side in the camps with, obviously, a great respect for one another's religion. In the United States we're so pitted in this so-called Holy War that we think people from two different religious have to war—it's not true.

DAN: Tell me about KINK-FM's role in this visit. What was the focus of your time in Ethiopia?

SHEILA: What they wanted me to do was go and meet the children who were orphaned by AIDS and talk to them about what their lives were like and to find out how it would be different if they were sponsored by World Vision. And boy, are they clear about it: they know who is sponsored and who isn't in these camps. The kids who are sponsored have pictures of Americans up on their mud huts and they have better clothes. Many of them are going to school. So for as hard as World Vision is pushing for equity in the camps, there is still an imbalance between those who are sponsored and those who aren't.

DAN: What was the goal for the alliance between KINK and World Vision?

SHEILA: We went over there with the idea that if we could get four hundred of these children sponsored that would be amazing. If we could do that, it would've been wildly successful. And I thought, *How in the world do you get a soccer mom, who is worried about public schools and her taxes, to care about a place on the other side of the world?* I was really skeptical that we could get four hundred sponsors. And I brought the interviews back and the phones started ringing and by the end of the day we had *eight hundred* people step forward and say, "We'll do this."

DAN: That's not bad for a heathen rock and roll station.

SHEILA: [laughs] Well, we're still heathens, but you know, we do care about other people's needs. I probably get an e-mail a day from someone who says, "I really wanted to take the time to evaluate what this World Vision trip was and read your blog and hear these stories, and now, three months later, I'm going to sign up and sponsor a child."

DAN: Wow.

SHEILA: Yeah, it's a great trickle-down effect; I'd say we're close to nine hundred kids by now.

DAN: How do you estimate what the need is?

SHEILA: Well, we fulfilled the need in Ethiopia. The kids that World Vision had identified as being orphaned and in need of sponsors have been fulfilled. If there were more calls from the KINK community, World Vision would have to match them up with another country.

DAN: Again, wow!

SHEILA: Yeah, it was really cool. Every kid that I met is basically taken care of until his or her eighteenth birthday.

DAN: How does that make you feel?

SHEILA: Fantastic! It makes me feel fantastic. How can you think about journalism in any other way except that, eventually, it's supposed to do good? But this is the first time in my career where there's been a cause and an effect. And if I could turn my career around and every story that I did could pose the problem and then offer the solution for people, I think it'd be magnificent change for the field.

DAN: You've been an Emmy Award-winning television journalist, and you've been in radio for years. How do you feel the media is doing in terms of bringing news, truth, and illumination to the public versus delivering entertainment dressed up like news?

SHEILA: I'm now really interested in how Christian causes are being covered in the media. For instance, I witnessed all these volunteers

in this Third World country doing the kind of work that I think
should be on television every single night. Who gets on? Jerry
Falwell, Pat Robertson, these people on the far extremes really
advocating hate, they're not advocating Christian values. And I
wish the news media could take a look at the gray areas, take a
look at the underbelly of what this movement is, who these
people are. They're basically soldiers doing really good work out
there. Maybe it's not a news story, but I think it's what people are
really hungry for.

DAN: The Body of Christ is the nickname for all the Followers in the
world trying to Jesus' work. Do you think people outside the
faith have an accurate perception of who Christians are?

SHEILA: I think it's probably wildly inaccurate. And that's because the
media does tend to polarize. I learned in television news you
can't deal in gray areas; so a story about a Christian who doesn't
hate his Muslim brother won't get the press. So there is a rub
there. I don't think people in the media mean to do that, I don't
think they intend to paint Christians as this archaic body of
people who are Bible thumping. But the truth is, people who get
press [laughs] are that way. It's true. I mean the number of times

even I will talk about what Pat Robertson says because it is so headline grabbing, how do you avoid it? But if every time I did that I balanced it with a story about a local mother who brought over a lasagna to a neighbor in her community who was diagnosed with breast cancer, we'd have a much more balanced picture of what Christian values are all about.

DAN: The loudest guys do seem to have taken the microphone, and it's interesting that the issues that seem to get the most play are the divisive ones. The gay issue and abortion, what else do you hear about?

SHEILA: But those are the issues that have become a political force in this country. I guess it's this politicization of Christianity that bothers me the most. I can't imagine Jesus choosing parties, saying, "Oh, yeah, I'm a Republican."

DAN: From your personal experience, you've seen a demonstration of His love and you've also heard the rhetoric based on, I guess, His point of view. Does one feel more true than another?

SHEILA: Oh yeah, seeing the work. Seeing the work is so profound. Because you see people wiping the flies from the eyes of these babies and dressing wounds of these infants who have exposed sores because they were given AIDS by their mothers. That work is so profound. It's so meaningful, you know? It's the kind of work that I don't know who else steps forward to do it. It seems to me that it's really true work.

DAN: Those volunteers you met, did they tell you why they were there?

SHEILA: The thing is, unless you ask they won't tell you. They're not saying, "Hey look, I'm digging this ditch and it's for Christ." They are very humble, which is another quality that absolutely thrilled me. We had to probe to find out why they were there: "It's Christ's work. We love Christ. This is what He'd want us to do. We're living in His vision and His eyes." I'm going to start crying. It's beautiful. It's just beautiful. You don't get to witness it in your daily life; that's why when you get an opportunity to see something so pure and so loving you just feel like you've been blessed too.

I have to tell you, I was so moved by Sheila's open heart, this interview really rattled me. For one, as she stated, Sheila is not a believer. But that didn't stop her from being able to recognize grace and sacrifice and all the other good work the volunteers were doing in Jesus' name. I loved that Sheila was generous enough and open enough to consider Christ in a new way, even though it contradicted what she thought a Christian was—or at least how Christ is represented by some with the microphone. It was inspiring that the beauty and strength of the demonstration of love that she saw in Africa was able to cut through all the crap Christianity shows her on a daily basis. That's how strong this faith is, that's how strong Jesus' love is. Sheila is a lovely woman with a big, beautiful heart and I can only pray that those within the faith will be as open to what she has to share as she was to us.

I was having coffee with my friend Phil—I say coffee but Phil always has tea—and we were talking about how Oregon was recently named the least religious state in America. I thought it was kind of funny because what does that mean anyway? I suppose we don't have the same institutional pressure to go to church as you may find back east with the Catholics or in the South with the Baptists, but that doesn't mean Oregon is full of Godless barbarians performing pagan rituals in the dense Northwestern woods. Oh, sure, we have that, too, but no more than anyplace else.

Anyway, Phil started telling me about something he saw on a Friday night under a bridge in downtown Portland. He saw a group of Christians get down on their hands and knees and wash the feet of homeless people. Yeah, and you thought the druids dancing in the forest was weird.

"They did what?" I demanded.

"Washed feet. They washed the feet of homeless people. I'd never seen anything like it," Phil said. "I cried watching them."

"Wow, did you do it too?"

"No, I couldn't. I just watched."

Phil had made quite a discovery. I'd never heard of this, but it turns out that every Friday night, under the Burnside Bridge in Portland's Old Town, Christians flood in from all over the state to meet the most basic needs of the city's homeless. In addition to providing food, clothing, and toiletries, these volunteers do something incredible . . . they provide respect, tenderness, and a human touch. There are lots of Christians who want to *do something*. This ministry, like others in every city in America, gives a forum where believers can show others what their faith is really about.

I met Marshall Snider, the founder of Bridgetown Ministries, at their northeast Portland headquarters in the late afternoon. Though sponsored by a church in the suburbs south of the city, they make their base camp in a derelict church fifteen minutes to the north. A core group of staffers and key volunteers sort clothing and supplies, prepare food, and load cars and trailers. Marshall delivered a brief and appropriate message on loving the lost as we shared a pregame meal together.

Around six in the evening, an army of volunteers began to straggle in, raising the energy level in the church basement considerably. There was an excitement, almost nervousness as believers from various area churches prepared to engage the homeless. A few had done this before, either on their own, with their home church, or with Bridgetown, but many hadn't—and it manifested in loud voices and jittery mannerisms.

Prior to departure, Marshall brought the group together for a few words. There must have been seventy or eighty people who had given up their Friday night to help someone in need. Marshall ran through a variety of cautions, courtesies, and house rules for Night Strike—the nickname for this operation.

"We're not here to preach. We want you to listen. We want each of you to learn someone's name tonight. If you aren't able to do anything else, learn somebody's name," he said.

I took note of that . . . don't preach? Interesting.

Next, Marshall explained the various jobs and called for volunteers: food serving, clothing distribution, set-up, water pourers, towel handlers.

I watched people confer with each other, raise hands, nod, and whisper as they made their decisions.

"As some of you know, one of the things we do, and we think it's pretty important, is wash feet. Who would like to wash feet tonight?" he asked.

The room became oddly still. A couple of hands shot up without hesitation—they've surely done this before and know something we don't know—

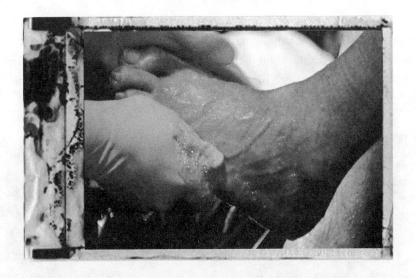

and then there was a pause. Marshall waited patiently. Before long a hand slowly went up, then another, then another. With all the positions filled Marshall led the group in prayer and we all departed for the city.

I arrived about twenty minutes to eight on this cool April night. The air was particularly damp as I surveyed the gray, dirty, empty parking space across from the MAX train tracks. *This can't be the spot,* I thought to myself. A homeless man sauntered over to me. "They're coming," he assured me.

"Who?" I asked, not wanting to make assumptions.

"The church people. They're here every Friday night." He smiled.

About ten minutes later two small trucks pulling trailers arrived, followed shortly by carload after carload of volunteers. With military precision, the trucks were emptied and suddenly that empty gray space looked like a tailgate party. Apparently, the name Night Strike refers to this swift transformation of empty lot to oasis.

It didn't take long for homeless and near-homeless people of all ages, shapes, and sizes to join the festivities. I watched from the edges and was surprised at the relaxed feel of the proceedings—it almost felt like I had stumbled onto a block party. Yes, this block party was full of people with torn and dirty clothing, yellow teeth and yellow eyes; some smelled of alcohol, but the smiling faces and buzz of conversation suggested a neighborhood barbeque, not an urban relief effort.

As the evening took shape Marshall hung back in a supervisory kind of role, allowing, no, subtly demanding, the volunteers carry the weight. The faithful nearly outnumbered those in need on this night, giving Marshall the latitude to enjoy catching up with a number of homeless folks he had come to know. He also had a few minutes to chat with me.

DAN: What the heck are you people doing down here tonight?
MARSHALL: We're trying to live out our mission statement which is to "Love people because people matter." Our focus is to love on people the way we think Jesus would love on people. These are the kind of places we think Jesus would show up, if He were here today. Bridgetown tries to provide an opportunity for the Body of Christ to come be the church rather than just go to church on a Sunday. Tonight we have about seventy volunteers from about ten to maybe fourteen different churches from all over Oregon. We've got Assemblies of God churches, Baptist churches, evangelical churches—all trying to be Jesus with skin on.

DAN: I see all kinds of tables set up; tell me about the specific needs you are filling here tonight.

MARSHALL: We have food, clothing, haircuts, a hair-washing station, the foot-washing stations . . . and what we call a dignity station, which is simply a mirror and a bowl of warm water so guys can shave—and we have tables set up for a living room atmosphere. We encourage the volunteers not just to come and serve people but to grab a bowl of food and sit down and eat with them, get to know their names. We want people to know Jesus, obviously, but, to be honest with you, we're really more interested in getting to know somebody's name first and then let the conversation go where the conversation goes. That's the heartbeat behind what we're trying to do. We want people to know that Jesus would sit at a table and eat with them. He wouldn't sit around and Bible-thump them or wave His finger at them or condemn them. Remember, Jesus hung out with the tax collectors and the prostitutes, and so we really feel like this is where He would be. And we see Him here in the eyes of the people.

DAN: For a lot of people today, thanks to some of the characters in the media creating a lot of sensation, the word *Christian* isn't necessarily a good word.

MARSHALL: Right. We feel like God put skin on and moved into the neighborhood and that's what we're trying to do, so we're saying this is what Christians are supposed to be about. And the word *Christian* means "Christ-like" or "little Christ." So if we're little-Christs, we're supposed to be apprenticed to Him. And so if they call you a Christian, I'm really hoping that it shows you're a Christian, they know you're a Christian because of your love, because of your actions rather than because you say some things or dogma or doctrine or read a certain kind of Bible. For us the action is a sacrament.

DAN: The "show me don't tell me" mentality can be so powerful and speaks so much louder than "the right verse."

MARSHALL: I know this is kind of cliché, but Saint Francis of Assisi said, "Preach the gospel and if necessary use words." More than anything this is just getting the Body of Christ out and loving on the culture. And then we find out we're not afraid of these people down here, the kind of people we normally lock our doors on, and now we're engaging in conversation with them.

DAN: What's the general feedback from those in need down here?

MARSHALL: Look around. They come down here to get hugged, get loved on, and hang out . . . we don't "bait and switch 'em" down here. We don't say, "You have to listen to our message before you eat." Our message is what we do; the food is part of the message, the conversation is part of the message, just hanging around is part of the message. I think they love it because it's not pushy, it's not in your face—not to say that's wrong, there's a place for all of that—but our message is more incarnational, more "with you," and we've been down here every Friday night for the past three years.

DAN: Let's talk about the foot-washing thing for a minute. That really struck me when I came down and visited before. I found that strangely powerful. How did you come to include that in your ministry?

MARSHALL: I was a youth pastor for fifteen years and in that fifteen years I went to all kinds of different things and I usually took my kids on these urban mission trips. And on one of those I went into San Francisco and they did one foot-washing station at this big square, and I felt that I was supposed to do that and so I washed feet. And I felt like I was supposed to wash feet without wearing gloves . . .

DAN: Now we're talking about washing the feet of the homeless and you were compelled to go without gloves?

MARSHALL: I grew up really poor and moving around a lot and, well, I just didn't like dirty people—let's put it that way. I was a dirty kid, that's how I grew up, and I struggled with that, knowing that's part of who I am. And so when I washed feet in San Francisco it really touched my life, kinda blasted me open—that was many years ago. In the Jewish culture, when you came in the door, part of the hospitality was to wash your feet. These guys are walking all day long and sometimes we'll change the same socks we put on last week. I think it's just a real humbling thing to do, to peel someone's socks off and just wash their feet with hot water and say, "Hey, can I pray with you, do you have any needs? We just want you to know you're special."

DAN: When I saw this I thought, *Yeah, that looks like something Jesus would do.* In fact, Jesus did do that. This seems familiar somehow.

MARSHALL: We're just really trying to do the best that we can to be about Jesus. I think that's what we need to be as Christians.

DAN: When you talk about this part of the ministry do people respond, "Yeah, great, I want to wash the feet of the homeless?"

MARSHALL: No, usually you have to stir them to do it. Some do, some don't. A lot of people think it's pretty radical. It's really not, I mean, you wash your feet every day, don't you?

DAN: I don't wash other people's feet and I don't, as a rule, wash homeless people's feet. You're just used to it.

MARSHALL: It's part of our living; it's not an event to us, I guess. We're just trying to be what Jesus wants us to be and I don't know how else to do it except this, right now, until God does something else.

I watched in amazement as a blonde woman in her forties led a skinny, weather-beaten man with wild gray hair to the foot-washing station. The man, probably in his sixties (but a case of "it's not the years it's the mileage"), settled into the chair, smoothing out his flannel shirt and lifting his feet in an effort to assist the blonde woman who was now pulling off his boots and filthy socks. The blonde woman, Denise, guided his feet into a warm bowl of water and gently massaged them. She talked quietly with the homeless man who occasionally leaned forward to compensate for the din from the nearby commuter train station, traffic on the overhead bridge, and echoes of other conversations.

They both patiently worked to find a place where both were comfortable enough to connect with each other. But the compassion displayed by Denise was so moving and such a clear expression of love for another of God's children that it was undeniable. I could see a true servant's heart on display and couldn't imagine how a person could fake something like that. It's one thing to write a check to your favorite charity; it's one thing to speak in sympathetic terms about the plight of those less fortunate; it's one thing to hand out blankets to homeless people; and it's *another* to get down on your hands and knees and lovingly wash the feet of a homeless person. To pour yourself into a simple act that says "I love you, you are special to me and to God."

Denise finished washing the homeless man's feet, slipped fresh clean socks on him, and laced up his boots for him. They shared a prayer together, hand in hand, before he left the chair and his female friend sat down with Denise.

Unable to resist, I intercepted this relaxed and grateful man on the way to the dinner table. Chuck told me (hey, I learned somebody's name), in rather basic terms, "The foot wash feels really good. Everybody likes that. I walk a lot, so it feels nice to have somebody do that for you." He had come to Night Strike several times and spoke in friendly, but relatively bland terms, about the kindness he received here, "Vicki and I can get a meal here, have people pray for us, get our feet washed, it's good."

As Chuck spoke, I realized that the volunteers here have achieved a remarkable success: Chuck felt deserving of the love—and considering how dehumanizing being on the street can be this was a major feat. Denise, Marshall and the other volunteers had made Chuck feel worthy, and he had taken them at their word: "I love you because Jesus loves you." It takes a genuine heart to make that sale.

After Chuck shuffled on to have dinner with friends, I visited with Denise. She herself had been homeless, on and off for years, and was now attending a church in Hood River, Oregon, that participates regularly in Night Strike. Denise explained she usually served the food because, "I'd been kind of uncomfortable and scared to do the feet. But tonight Marshall said, 'If you feel uncomfortable, if you're broke and you're tired, you need to do the thing that you don't want to do.' At first I didn't think I could do it, but I learned last week and did a couple and people just love it. He said tonight, 'If you ever feel uncomfortable, just pretend you are washing Jesus' feet.'"

"It seems like a pretty humbling thing to wash someone's feet," I offered.

"It is. I know what it's like to be there on the streets," Denise's voice trailed off and she began to cry. She hid behind her ball cap for a moment before managing to speak loudly enough for me to hear, "More than food and everything, people crave hugs and touches." She wiped her eyes, and then the strength returned to her voice. "The hardest part for me is that we have to use gloves, because when you're already on the street you feel like you're dirty and nobody wants to touch you. More than food, people crave touch and hugs." She smiled at me through her tears.

"I think you passed on a real blessing to the people you served tonight."

"It's a real blessing to me that the church allows me to do this," she smiled. "Vicki and Chuck were the first people I washed last week, and they asked me to start praying for them. They were really humbled, and they wanted our prayers. They're a wonderful couple, and Vicki didn't want me to stop." Denise laughed.

I wondered if a person can do an act like this with some other motivation in mind or if, as I assumed, as I hoped, it was something that can't be faked.

"I pray for Jesus to purify my heart before I do this. Because if you are a Christian and you are doing it just because you want the blessing, you're not gonna get blessed. You've got to go into this saying, 'I want to do this Jesus whether you bless me or not.' If you remember the Last Supper, the last thing Jesus did was wash the feet of all His disciples."

There's that "Jesus with skin on" thing again.

Denise then caught me off guard with a question. "Can I wash your feet?"

Honestly, I wasn't sure how to react. I didn't want my feet washed, I guess I'm a little self-conscious and I surely

don't consider my feet to be my most attractive feature. But the last thing I wanted to do was be discouraging to this kind and sweet woman. And then I wondered why my initial reaction was to cover up, to stay private, to stay separate from another.

"Sure. Why not?" I heard myself say.

I took a page from Marshall's book and imagined that Jesus was going to wash my feet. *Jesus loves me: He wouldn't make fun of my twisted middle toe; He won't grimace if my nails are too long.* I suppressed my embarrassment as I pulled off my socks and slipped off my shoes. I was surprised that such a simple action was making me so twitchy.

Having your feet washed is actually quite a comforting, if unusual experience. The warm water felt great, the tender touch was soothing, but I didn't feel worthy of such treatment. Foot-washing may be as difficult for the receiver as it is for the giver. Of course, the superficial unpleasantness of washing another's feet (particularly a foot in desperate need of cleansing) is quite obvious but, strangely, the role of receiver was far more difficult than I would've imagined. And, here's the funny part, it actually reminded me of something: God and me. This foot-washing thing is a great metaphor to grasping God's grace, His gift of life that we haven't earned. As Denise lathered liquid soap and then moisturizer on my feet I was continually repealing my embarrassment and shame over imperfect feet, jagged toenails, and calloused skin. I tried to accept her gift without disqualifying myself as unworthy. It struck me that this reflex is actually a form of selfishness or self-centeredness as my instinct was to reject this blessing I hadn't earned.

Denise didn't share my concerns, her desire was to deliver the gift. God too, chooses to see past my by brokenness when He offers me grace. I wondered how many times I have rejected His gifts, His guidance, His love because I wasn't willing simply to be open to Him. Yeah, I know, this foot-washing business is pretty profound.

I have to tell you I'm tickled by the fact that both of these stories originated in godless Portland, the least religious state in the country. So much for the easy labeling of others, eh? I'm getting pretty comfortable with something Tony Campolo told me: "We're never as right as we think we are; we're never as wrong as we think we are." I suppose if this outpouring of love, kindness, and consideration is happening in such strange and beautiful forms in godless Portland, then I have hope. How cool that loving-kindness actually works.

Chapter Fourteen

the sea refuses
N O R I V E R

The sea refuses no river.

I've always liked going to the ocean. As a kid, my brothers and cousins would splash around like idiots, squealing and screaming in the cold Pacific surf. The chilly water would feel bone-crushing at first, but as the numbness set in we didn't care anymore and would play for hours. As I grew up my fondness for the sea developed and matured, and I found it a place where I could clear my head and reenergize my spirit. I don't really understand how it worked, but going to the ocean would revitalize me. Perhaps it was the way the sun would cut through the dramatic clouds at the Oregon coast; maybe it was the glow of the gorgeous and surprising emerald-green water accented by the gleaming white foam, which in turn melts into the gray sand. Throw in that fresh, salty breeze and the constant, reassuring rumble of the sea dancing to and fro and I'm set.

My wife and I walk the beach and every few minutes one of us calls out, "Look at the beauty, just look at it." Standing on the shoreline looking over swelling waves that stretch to the horizon, I am left in awe. I just can't deny I'm part of something vast and amazing. I'm a tiny little part to be sure, but somehow, for me, I feel connected to it all when I feel that salty air kiss my face while I'm being hypnotized by the rocking of the sea.

The sea refuses no river.

Since I was about fifteen I haven't been able to look at the sea and not hear selections from the Who's rock opera *Quadrophenia*. You see, the climax of the story takes place at the sea with the epic song "Love Reign O'er Me," where the main character, Jimmy, a mod teen, has tried to fill his God-shaped hole with pills, girls, conforming to a gang, fighting, and is finally at the end of his rope. Jimmy steals a scooter, drives like a demon until he runs out of real estate at the shore—broken, lost, hopeless, and out of ideas. He just sits there on the rocks looking out at the sea. The only answer the sea gives is a prompt skyward, where Jimmy calls out to God. He prays, essentially, "God, if you're really there, please, please, rain. Rain your love down on me." And a funny thing happens . . . it rains. The rain pours down, symbolically washing Jimmy's sins clean and redeeming him. How cool is it that a message of forgiveness, surrender, and hope comes wrapped up in rock opera by one of rock's most notorious bands. I'm sure there are smarter literary allusions involving God and the sea; Hemingway and Melville come to mind, but neither of them could windmill a power chord while scissor-kicking across the stage and then smash a telecaster to bits on stage . . . so I'm going to stick with Pete Townshend. For years I wondered if I was reading God into the seemingly obvious symbolism because it lined up neatly with my belief system, but I saw Townshend interviewed once and that's almost exactly how he described it. Sometimes you call out to God and He answers, which leaves you with one question: "What are you going to do about it?"

The sea refuses no river.

At the end of our *Lord, Save Us From Your Followers* documentary, there's a beautiful song called "Come Home Sweet Child" that plays under the images of the many people I met on this journey. The melody is gorgeous and emotive; it will break your heart and put it back together again, and underscores the goodwill and kind hearts exchanged along the way. The lyrics are lovely and tender and seem to call out to the faces of the wonderful children of God who shared something of themselves with me. When my associate producer, Matt, showed me his first rough cut of the "Come Home Sweet Child" montage, I choked up. Jimmy and I must've cut four or five versions, refining the

piece, hitting certain moments, and that, my friends, took days and days of work . . . and still I choke up. I've probably sat through the movie a dozen or so times by now and when the montage comes around . . . hand me the hanky. Shoot, Sam's song came up on my iTunes shuffle last night and I could feel my heart swell, my throat tighten, and eyes mist.

The song is truly beautiful and I'm sure you'd like it, but it's also really personal to me. When I first heard it, I was driving home from twelve or fourteen or sixteen mind-numbing hours in the edit suite with Jimmy. I popped the CD into the player. Sam had seen a rough cut of the film and created some songs for me to sample. It had been a couple of weeks and I just hadn't made time to listen to his work. I had been too consumed with finishing the movie and, in particular, ending the film. The movie demands a lot from the viewer both intellectually and emotionally (at least it did from me, you can judge for yourself). At the end of the arduous edit I was struggling for an ending beat, a moment where the audience could feel what I felt on this journey. I want people to reflect, contemplate, and think about these issues—but I really want them to *feel*. Not everybody can take two years out of his or her life to meet and talk to all these people like I did, but I sure wanted to share the benefit from it and part of that is just feeling different in your own skin. But after this journey, how do I put a bow on it? How do I say, "There . . . like that, it feels something like that."

There were something like eight or ten tracks on Sam's *Lord, Save Us . . .* demo CD, all the songs creative, interesting, and compelling in their own way. I listened to a minute or two of each song and then skipped ahead to the next. These were good songs, mind you, but nothing grabbed me as right for the film . . . until track six that is. The song opens with a sweeping, majestic keyboard and an insistent beat that immediately grabbed me . . . and then Sam begins to sing. There was something enchanting about the melody and I began to see pictures . . . faces and places from my journey swirling through my head in time with the music. Then when the chorus hit I literally erupted in tears while driving down I-5. I'm serious, I had a full-on, spontaneous,

volcanic, emotional meltdown the very first time I listened to "Come Home Sweet Child." I praised God, I begged forgiveness, I sang at the top of my lungs and saw the end of the movie materialize before me—all in two minutes and fifty-three seconds.

I hit the button on my steering wheel and the song began again. Specific images from my journey popped into my head—Al Franken laughing, Rick Santorum grinning, Mike in Dealey Plaza explaining the JFK conspiracy to me, Denise washing the feet of a homeless man, Sister Mary Timothy smiling sweetly, shaking hands with a Jimi Hendrix impersonator, laughing with Lou in Times Square at one in the morning, and so many more. What a gift this little song was to me. Something magical and heavenly in the notes and lyrics released the idea I had sought and it's a sweet coda that encapsulates two years of discovery for me. I think my joy in hearing this song, though, was realizing it would be possible for people to watch this movie and feel what I felt. Sam's song could carry my heart's cry, supporting the images in a way that my words never could.

Come Home Sweet Child
by Sam Martin

I know what your soul looks like
After all I designed it myself
I created the sky above
And everything you can and can't see
Come Home My Child
I've loved you all your life
Come Home Sweet Child
I've never left your side . . . all this time
I want to give you that peace you're looking for
Even if you've been knocking on the wrong doors

I love you the way you are
No matter what you have done
Fall back and depend on me
And my love will set you free

Come Home My Child
I've loved you all your life
Come Home Sweet Child
I've never left your side . . . all this time
I want to give you that peace you're looking for
Even if you've been knocking on the wrong doors

It's funny. Some of these people only shared a couple of minutes of their time and will have totally forgotten about the idiot in the bumper-sticker suit, but I won't forget them. Each and every person who was willing to connect with me, even for a few minutes, gave me a gift, gave me encouragement that has enormous value. I guess they gave me proof that we're not condemned to suffer antipathy and division. I'm encouraged we can do better, we all want to do better anyway, and if we make the effort to get out of our own way a little bit, our ability to connect with each other will come easier. And I gotta tell you, I met lots of people who didn't share my beliefs, but it was a wonderful feeling to hang out, share a laugh, and connect. It reminded me of my brothers and cousins splashing gleefully in the ocean, consumed by something larger than us. I know we're both children of God. If they don't know it shouldn't change anything for me and I know it doesn't change anything for God.

There's a lot about faith and God and love that I don't quite understand. I'm okay with the fact that "full, complete, perfect love" is beyond my reach and beyond the reach of this world. I know I'm probably limited to grasping sand-sized bits of understanding, but I'm grateful for those little bits. Each and every one of the meetings, conversations, and interactions I had along this journey brought me so many grains of sand closer to understanding what real love is.

The sea refuses no river.

I'm back at the beach. I stroll along in the sunshine until I reach the inlet for the Little Nestucca river, which (truth be told) is not much of a river, really. Perhaps farther up river it's something grand, but here, where it meets the mighty Pacific, it's only a piddling eight inches deep and fifty feet across.

How is it that something so minor, so insignificant, is received by something so epic? The Pacific Ocean sure doesn't need the Nestucca, it's not going to dry up without this trickle, and yet it is accepted, welcomed into the infinite sea. I watched this stream fold under and flow into the breaking waves and saw a glimpse of God and me. In that moment, something foundational was revealed in the water: if I come to Him, openly, simply, honestly seeking, I will be welcomed home. I don't have to be perfect or even good; if I surrender I know I will not be refused, I understand that. It also seems as if the closer to God I get, the more I want to be good, not because I'm afraid of wrath and judgment, but because I understand His grace for me more clearly and *I want to love Him like He loves me.* It's depressing to think of trying to be good enough to earn God's love—I don't know how that lie began, but I watch the truth splash around in front of me, as the endless sea accepts the river.

There are lots of days when I feel like the river trying to make its way back to the sea. Once in a while I do feel the embrace of the ocean; other days I feel like I'm starting off at the top of the mountain once again. But as I watch the sun dance across the waves I have this reassuring, palpable feeling that there *are* answers to *all* the questions. I have way more questions than answers, but really, we're talking about the minutiae of life, aren't we? I'm at peace with the big answers: God made me and everyone else special, He loves me, He wants me to love everyone else, and there's lots of other stuff going on all around me that I'm only sorta clued in on. And simply knowing the answers exist is oddly comforting. The answers come when they come, you know? Well, come to think of it, the answers seem to arrive at some mysterious interval *after* the question is asked.

Acknowledgments

First and foremost I would like to thank my family. I know what you're thinking, "Didn't he already dedicate the book to Kara, Nick, and Nate?" Yeah, I did, and yeah, they're that good.

Thanks to everybody at Lightning Strikes Entertainment. The intrepid J-Man (you gotta love a guy with a nickname) and the indefatigable Jim Standridge. Thanks to Jon Manning, Aaron Cohen, Terry Hoffman, Matt Miadich, and Matt Conners for helping the adventure stick to tape.

Special thanks to the entire Thomas Nelson family: a tip of the hat to Matt Baugher, who put his money (er, Thomas Nelson's money) where his mouth was and became our first champion, and to David Moberg, who was our second; to Thom and the Chittom Family Players for their dedication and vacation-marathon editing; Kay for beautifully crafting the book's visual motif; nice job spreading the word by Emily, Kristi, Stephanie; and thanks to Beth, Randy, Lisa, Steve, and the rest of the road warriors for doing what they do!

Some people take inspiration from their co-conspirators. I call mine INSPIRATORS! Much thanks to: Jonathon Komack-Martin, Mike Mercer, Erik Lokkesmoe, Kevin Palau, Bob Arnold, Gabe Lyons, Michael Donaldson, Josh Butler, Ranjy Thomas, Ray Nelson, Bill Reeves, Dan Merrell, Rich Peluso, Steve Okin, John Bauman, Matt Crouch, Rich Cook, Joe Anaya, Doug Hostetter, Eric Wiler, Tim Larson, Tony Kriz, Paul Metzger,

Acknowledgments

Tony Hall, Marta and Demi, Neguissie, Tom Krat, Tom Newman, Ian Hamilton, Steve Karakas, Rod and Teresa Koop, Steve Mitchell, Mark Nicklas, Randy Remington, Steve Kenny, Kip Jacobs, Reid Smith, The Crane Family Foundation, Dale Ebel, Rick Warren, Rob Bell, Craig Gross, Mike Foster, James Melkonian, who knows how to Rock Out Full Tilt Boogie Style better than anyone I know, Gunnar Simonsen, who is THE man, to Sam, Bruce, Bono, Mick and Keith, Rog and Pete, The Hip and The Bosshouse boys—keep it rockin'!

My deepest gratitude for all those who sat for interviews, who visited with Bumper-Sticker Man, who listened when they felt like talking, who chose to smile when it was easier to scowl, who opened their hearts and risked it all. May God bless you.